# Literacy Learning Communities

*A Guide for Creating Sustainable Change in Secondary Schools*

R E L E A H  C O S S E T T  L E N T

D1397861

H E I N E M A N N  PORTSMOUTH, NH

**Heinemann**
A division of Reed Elsevier Inc.
361 Hanover Street
Portsmouth, NH 03801-3912
www.heinemann.com

*Offices and agents throughout the world*

**Library of Congress Cataloging-in-Publication Data**
Lent, ReLeah Cossett.
    Literacy learning communities : a guide for creating sustainable change in secondary schools / ReLeah Cossett Lent.
        p. cm.
    Includes bibliographical references and index.
    ISBN-13: 978-0-325-01122-6
    ISBN-10: 0-325-01122-2
    1. School improvement programs—United States.  2. School environment—United States.  3. Teachers—Professional relationships—United States.
4. Teachers—In-service training—United States.  5. Language arts
(Secondary)—United States.  I. Title.

LB2822.82.L45 2007
373.12—dc22                                        2007016388

*Editor:* Leigh Peake
*Production service:* Denise A. Botelho
*Production coordinator:* Lynne Costa
*Cover design:* Catherine Hawkes, Cat & Mouse
*Typesetter:* Eric Rosenbloom, Kirby Mountain Composition
*Manufacturing:* Jamie Carter

Printed in the United States of America on acid-free paper
11  10  09  08  07   EB   1  2  3  4  5

*To Gloria Pipkin,*
*whose friendship*
*has always*
*sustained me.*

*Why does trust matter? Because relationships matter, especially in the business of schooling. Our work touches that most elusive part of the human spirit, and our greatest rewards often appear as intangible flickers of learning that cross the faces of those in our classrooms each day. When a faculty creates a culture of trust, it immerses all its members, including students, in an environment where relationships have the potential of turning knowledge into wisdom.*

*Perhaps the only true commonality that schools share is that they are each unique. Every student added to the student body, every teacher added to the faculty, every new administrator and staff member changes the complexion of the school. Every program, course, or extra-curricular activity adds a shade that alters the school's impressionistic feel. . . . Each literacy learning community, then, is born from its own schoolwide community and must enter this new world of professional development by recognizing and honoring the unique environment that produced it.*

# Contents

# *Acknowledgments*

Even as I pen the words *trust*, *respect*, and *caring* to describe learning communities, I realize that the reason I know about those characteristics is because of the colleagues, friends, and family who have brought them to life for me. It occurred to me as I was reflecting on my own communities that they, like most good things, come in various sizes and shapes. For example, Walton District Schools, a small, close-knit district where I have been a literacy consultant for several years, helped me grow in ways that can only occur where you have grown comfortable. I learned as I worked with teachers and principals who opened their classrooms and shared their students, and I was nurtured through the secondary literacy coaches who welcomed me as a part of their own learning community.

Another of my communities was made up of colleagues and friends who formed a circle around me as I struggled with fitting all the parts of this book together. Leigh Peake, my editor, trusted me enough to support and encourage my endeavors in this, a book that didn't seem to fit in any prescribed niche. Her astute comments and wise insights helped shape my thoughts into a coherent whole. Gloria Pipkin, my dear friend who also happens to be a talented editor, is *always* on the mark and has this uncanny ability to tell me what my subconscious has been saying all along. Susan Kelly was willing to read parts of the evolving manuscript and give me her unvarnished opinion, even when I was telling her secrets. Connie Cain, Cheree Davis, Christy Williamson, and April Johnson allowed me to tap into their experiences with learning communities when I needed concrete examples.

Although families are supposed to be supportive and encouraging, and mine certainly is, a few members of my family went beyond the call of familial duty. Both my husband, Bert, and my father, Don Cossett, read every word of this manuscript and gave me valuable advice and hours of their time. Bert, the patient saint that he is, had to listen to me read a chapter aloud before reading it carefully himself. If he happened to miss anything, my father, with his engineer's mind, caught it. Sometimes they even ganged up on me—insisting, for example, that a particular word simply wasn't quite right or a concept needed "unpacking." They also forgot that I was once an English teacher and tried to talk me into placing commas where *they* thought they should go.

Other family members also helped make the chapters unfold. Bert's father, while visiting at Christmas, read and responded thoughtfully to chapters. My sister Kristy, a wonderful teacher in her own right, helped me understand various models of professional learning communities and put me in touch with her colleagues, Pam Peters in particular, who took time from her busy day as a principal to talk to me about how she facilitated professional learning communities (PLCs) in her school.

I also appreciate the fine professionals at Heinemann who turned my pages into a real book, especially Lynne Costa, my production editor.

It does indeed take a village, otherwise known as a learning community, to raise a child, but it also takes one to write a book. For all of my communities, I am grateful.

# Introduction

Community, not curriculum, is where many of our
improvement efforts now need to be focused.

—ANDY HARGREAVES

When I first met my husband and he learned that I was a teacher, he took me to an elementary school in the northern Florida Panhandle. His job as an environmentalist had required that he visit the school on more than one occasion, and he told me that he was always taken with the "feel" of Carr Elementary School. It was what a school should be like, he said, although he didn't know a thing about elementary curriculum, scientifically based reading research, or adequate yearly progress. "There's something about the way the principal treats the teachers," he said. "Everyone is always smiling, and the teachers' warmth toward the kids is obvious. The place just seems like where you would want your child to spend his day. There is a sense of community that is palpable." I didn't know much about elementary schools at that time, either, but when I visited the school, I understood. A school's community can't be mandated, graded, or even enforced, but it can be created, nurtured, and sustained through the conscious efforts of everyone within that community.

For years, many schools, especially secondary schools, didn't give much thought to community when they considered the school's culture. They wanted to make sure the school ran like a well-oiled machine, and each person had a part to play in the mechanical workings. There were master schedules, credits, and sports programs to consider. There were safety issues, curriculum goals, and standards. And then, almost as an afterthought, there was professional development. If districts could nab a motivating and engaging speaker to fire teachers up, especially at the beginning of the school year, they felt they had wisely spent their professional development dollars. Teachers rarely had any input into the topic, and the sessions were often far removed from the daily workings of the classroom. *Training* was the word most closely associated with professional development, and community was where one lived, not where one worked. Unfortunately, few people asked how the training increased student learning. Teachers were required to gain inservice credit, however, so they sat, received their training, and then went back to their classrooms and did the best they could with what had been given to them.

During the past several years, however, staff development has morphed from a passive saturation of information to interactive communication in the form of professional learning communities. Joyce and Showers, in *Student Achievement Through Staff Development* (2002), Michael Fullan in *Breakthrough* (Fullan, Hill, and Crevola 2006), and The Alliance for Excellent Education all show unequivocal research results: High quality professional development with embedded support positively affects student learning and improves standardized test scores. A Policy Research Brief produced by the National Council of Teachers of English on Adolescent Literacy Reform offers quotes such as the following that are typical of the findings: "A growing body of research documents the connection between systematic and sustained professional development and improved student achievement" (2006, 11). Research also confirms that professional collaboration is essential to success. In fact, Joyce and Showers (2002) document that when peer coaching is added to the training components of theory, demonstration, and practice, the transfer of knowledge to the classroom increases from 0 percent to 95 percent.

Unfortunately, while the research is branded into policies at district and state education offices, many schools do not have the time, knowledge, or logistical underpinnings to offer the type of professional development that will most benefit their students. It is one thing to mandate that staff development be sustained, embedded, and ongoing, but how, exactly, are these transformations to occur? Enter the latest educational buzzwords:

coaching and professional learning communities. As is so often the case in bureaucratic thinking, once the term exists, the problem appears to be solved. Too many schools have bought into the terminology but have been unable to embrace the concept.

In much the same way, literacy has been addressed by invoking the word *strategies*, one that has permeated every classroom corner. Teachers who never thought much about reading, especially secondary content-area teachers, have been suddenly immersed in a new language that ranges from acronyms such as K-W-Ls, to terms pulled straight from elementary reading classes, such as *fluency probes*, and *phonemic awareness*.

The flood of scientifically based literacy research has prompted districts to offer ubiquitous workshops on literacy in the content area, especially in schools and districts desperately needing teachers deemed "highly qualified." Often there is little follow-up or support because of the enormity of the initiative. To some extent, technology has revamped "sit and get" professional development, but other problems have emerged. Teachers spend their planning periods at their computers engaged in online literacy courses, providing evidence that they are proficient by participating in cyberchats, but many then retreat to the sanctuary of their classrooms for business as usual. Often this computer-based professional development exacerbates the problem of isolationism and emphasizes content over collaboration.

There is little doubt that most reading coaches and district staff developers understand the importance of helping teachers find literacy practices relevant to their content areas, but federal and state bureaucrats have been so insistent that everyone get on board the literacy train quickly that whole districts often leave the station without knowing where they are headed. Predictably, teachers have resisted such a journey imposed by those who don't seem to understand secondary content-area studies or the developmental needs of adolescents. And worse, they haven't been given the time to build community, examine learning needs, study current research, or apply literacy instructional practices that support content area subjects.

When under pressure, teachers who know better often feel they have no choice but to rely on quick fixes, as demonstrated by the massive test-prep practices that have infused classrooms all across America. Even the progressive notion of literacy coaching too often bends to data-driven, as opposed to data-informed, practices in a race for quantifiable results. In many cases, embedded staff development has given way to workshops designed solely to show teachers how to increase test scores.

Fortunately, many secondary schools have rejected this obsolete model of professional development and their students have made significant progress in learning due to embedded staff development utilizing learning communities and peer coaching. The concept of professional learning communities, however, is more likely to be found in elementary schools than in secondary schools because elementary schools are smaller, the emphasis is often placed on the development of the child rather than mastery of content, and the community is inherently closer since schools represent neighborhoods rather than large geographical areas. Secondary schools, on the other hand, are faced with several inherent challenges to collaborative learning. Isolation, the antithesis of community, is intrinsic to large departmentalized schools as teachers and students alike tend to spend time in clubs, academic areas, or groups with others who have common interests or social or ethnic similarities. In many high schools, teachers may not have even one in-depth conversation with another staff member, much less a professional dialogue. Some teachers report that they have to refer to the yearbook to remind them who teaches what. This culture of fragmentation, which is as much a part of the secondary environment as proms and car washes, does not encourage or sustain schoolwide professional learning. Even when the principal understands the importance of establishing a cohesive learning community, awareness and implementation are two very different realities.

With this book, then, I am seeking to provide teachers, administrators, and district personnel with research-based theories and specific tools for their work within a community, whether with a partner or within a larger group at the school or in the district. In addition, I have provided readers with ways of interlacing literacy and community in a manner that supports content area instruction within interdependent teams of learners.

Section 1, "Creating an Environment for Literacy Learning," begins by showing the unambiguous research supporting collaborative professional learning and its compelling effect on student learning. Included is a frank discussion on the importance of relationship and trust as foundational tools for sustained and effective communities. The final chapter in Section 1 asks readers to broaden their definitions of literacy to include multiple and digital literacies, both of which are integral to the lives of our students, but have yet to make their way into the curriculums of many schools.

Section 2, "Building a Community for Literacy Learning," provides a nuts-and-bolts approach that gets down to the business of creating an initial literacy learning community (LLC) that will guide the formation of other learning communities as they spawn from the original. Tools are provided to help learning communities assess their literacy needs through formal and informal data collection and analysis. The last chapter in Section 2, "Developing a Literacy Learning Plan," will provide LLCs with several concrete examples of literacy learning plans, complete with resources to guide them in the development of their own customized plans of action. This section offers a three-year plan for authentic, sustained, and embedded staff development that targets the entire school community, including students.

The final section, "Developing Tools for Literacy Learning," guides faculties in instituting the powerful collaborative practices of study groups, coaching, and action research to support whole-school literacy efforts. Each of these professional development tools will reinforce and expand the work of literacy learning communities and may be adapted for student use as well.

At the end of each chapter, I have included "Questions for Reflection," prompts that will allow individuals and small groups to make personal connections to the concepts presented in the chapter through either writing or dialogue. There is also a section at the end of each chapter titled "Reflection Through Action" that suggests activities for small groups of teachers, LLCs, administrators, or district staff development personnel to use in expanding and customizing collaboration, again often including students or the wider surrounding community. Finally, I offer books related to the topic of each chapter that may be used for deeper learning in study-group sessions.

As the school shifts from isolated pods of teachers and students to a cohesive learning community, it will begin the rewarding, vitalizing task of weaving literacy knowledge into the fabric of its daily life. Literacy coaches, teachers, principals, and district staff will have access to current research and practical tools as they help each other move into an era of enriched learning and collaboration, an era that will transform staff development from a remnant of the past into an intrinsically rewarding professional experience that will benefit students and teachers alike.

*Section One*

# Creating an Environment for Literacy Learning

Words. Words that allow us to communicate, to
reach out, to touch each other if only verbally. And
the other side of words, where we find silence.

—ROBERT CORMIER, *I HAVE WORDS TO SPEND:*
*REFLECTIONS OF A SMALL-TOWN EDITOR*

A classroom environment, like a home environment, speaks in unmistakable voices about its occupants. It's all there for even the most casual visitor to discern, from the teacher's sense of organization to the student's level of comfort. The environment of the school is equally transparent, and even intangible components, such as trust, collegiality, and respect are evident immediately. Of course, positive and nurturing environments sometimes are created by the luck of the draw—a knowledgeable, collaborative staff finds itself partnered with a principal who understands the complexities of leadership, and the rest is history. Most of the time, however, a learning community within a classroom, school, or district must be cultivated through the building of relationships, a commitment to the truth, and a driving desire for knowledge.

This section addresses questions that will set the stage for building authentic, embedded, and sustained literacy learning communities.

*Why does community matter?*

*Why does trust matter?*

*Why does literacy learning matter?*

# Why Community Matters

We rarely talk with each other about teaching at any depth—
and why should we when we have nothing more than
"tips, tricks, and techniques" to discuss? That kind of talk
fails to touch the heart of a teacher's experience.

—PARKER PALMER, *THE COURAGE TO TEACH*

The science teacher looked at me and smiled, his lips forming a compliant response to my comment. I wondered if it were biologically possible to smile and grimace at the same time. I felt I was being completely ineffective in my role as "professional developer" for this teacher, even though he was responding with all the appropriate motions—nodding at regular intervals, turning to the page in the book I was referencing, making eye contact, and listening respectfully. I was not buying it, however. I had been a teacher for too many years to be fooled by politeness, although there were days in the classroom that I would have traded just about anything for it. I know that politeness is often an effective cover for disagreement or, worse, indifference.

I was discouraged because I was trying to do all the right things. I had been hired as a literacy consultant by the district to spend several days throughout the year with science teachers on content-area literacy. The previous year I had helped schools in this same district form reading leadership teams and many of the science teachers had served on these same teams, so this was hardly a "sit and get," one-shot model of professional development. I had been in these teachers' classrooms; the principal had provided time for professional study; and I saw my role more as coach than professional developer as I supported teachers in implementing new

**3**

instructional practices. Nevertheless, I felt myself becoming flustered at the robotic responses of this teacher, and I knew I was trying too hard to break through his courteous veneer. Finally, I looked him square in the eyes and said, "Can we talk about this?" I wasn't surprised to find that he knew exactly what I wanted to discuss.

*so many!*

"Well, since you asked . . . here's the issue. My students can read but I don't expect them to read every day," he responded, matter-of-factly. "This is a science class, not a reading class. The students need to understand and use the scientific process, and I provide the content in a way that engages them, such as through PowerPoint presentations. I have to prepare them for their next science course and for the state standardized science test, and I believe that I am doing a good job of that."

"But how will they be able to become better science readers if you're not giving them lots of opportunities to read science text of all types? How will they become successful science students in the future if you don't teach them *how* to approach science text? Someone may not always be there to give them the content," I countered.

"I made it all the way through college without reading chapters in the textbook or reading every word of a scientific article. In science we learn by doing—students don't have to read every day to learn science. I've been teaching science a long time, and my students have learned a lot from me throughout the years."

It was clear that we had become partners in a professional development dance that I had hoped was not a part of my repertoire. Fortunately, I realized what was happening before the music ended, and we went on to have a deep, thoughtful, and reflective professional dialogue. I had stumbled into one of the pitfalls of traditional professional development by assuming the role of a literacy "expert" without taking the time to become a learner first. I assumed that this teacher was following closely behind me as I led him to literacy enlightenment. If I had been walking with him, instead of leading the way, I might not have traveled so far alone. Ultimately, this teacher caused me to think about my long-held beliefs about academic reading, which, in turn, led me to engage in meaningful conversations with other colleagues working in content-area literacy. I even interviewed the science teacher's students in my quest to better understand his ideas.

In any case, I abandoned Plan A, which was *my* plan to help him utilize various instructional practices designed to help students learn to read science text. Because I had not factored in his teaching experience, content expertise, and the context in which he worked each day, his time with me had not translated into increased student learning in literacy, and that is simply not acceptable. I am now looking forward to our next meeting and hope that our individual thinking has shifted enough to allow each of us to gain new perspectives as we study current research and examine his students' data, both formal and informal. I am optimistic that our candid dialogue will lead us to a mutual understanding about the role of reading in science classes.

> High-quality staff development is founded on a sense of collegiality and collaboration among teachers and between teachers and principals in solving important problems related to teaching and learning.
>
> —Dennis Sparks, past executive director, National Staff Development Council

Time is too valuable to waste on placating professional developers, district personnel, principals, or consultants. Each teacher deserves the opportunity to engage in differentiated professional learning based on his or her strengths and weaknesses as well as the needs of the students. I could provide all the "tips, tricks, and techniques" in my bag, but information, no matter how well researched or scientifically based, that lacks a meaningful connection with a human learner becomes impotent. This is the critical lesson we have learned from our work with students, and it applies to adult learners as well.

*how many students feel*

Despite the challenges that occurred during my time at this high school, the professional development experience was probably more productive than staff development most schools experienced in the past. We've come a long way from the days when traditional professional development was laid out months, even years, in advance, the topic predetermined based on "what's hot" or more likely, who's available, with the district inservice calendar neatly filled in with topics and presenters. If they were lucky, teachers could choose an interesting subject at a centralized location, but more often professional development would be delivered at the school site, one workshop fitting all. I have attended staff development meetings in school media centers where administrators hovered around the perimeter of the room like guards watching rowdy inmates, while teachers covertly graded papers or wrote lesson plans, surreptitiously checking off one more item in their never-ending list of job duties. The presenter alternatively entertained, motivated, taught, or facilitated, but the handouts were inevitably filed away in cabinets, even when bound in brightly colored paper or accompanied with a jazzy CD or videotape. The follow-up, if it occurred at all, may have been an exercise in fragmentation and superficiality, such as asking teachers to write a paragraph telling their department heads how they planned to use "something they learned" in order to fulfill the district's professional development requirements. In more progressive districts, teachers may have been asked to provide documentation in the form of student data that dug a bit deeper into the presented topic, but the option for authentic, collaborative learning was lost once the form was turned over to the designated professional development overseer.

Traditional professional development relied on an isolated event that interrupted, but rarely supported, classroom learning. In fact, many teachers would schedule doctors' appointments on inservice days, when classes were suspended, rather than have to deal with planning lessons for substitutes on days when students were in school. Some districts even allowed teachers to take comp time on inservice days, especially when teachers had attained their required inservice points. Teachers who had racked up hours (and weeks and months) of overtime looked forward to the break, often coming to school anyway to tie up classroom loose ends when the kids were not underfoot. Inevitably, athletic coaches found important tasks in the gym resulting in their missing inservice sessions. Principals would make an appearance to welcome the presenter or pop in to show his or her support, and then disappear to take care of the important business of running the school. Professional development, like so many well-intentioned educational initiatives, became a bureaucratic exercise that interfered with teachers' busy schedules and often had little to do with the students or instructional practices in real classrooms.

Even when teachers learned new information in professional development workshops, research began to confirm what we knew all along: the knowledge gained by teachers in such sessions rarely transferred to classroom practice or increased student learning because teachers were not using their new knowledge in the classroom. This isolated, top-down model of professional development wasted the time, talents, and good will of millions of teachers.

Bruce Joyce and Beverly Showers' (2002) research on professional learning transformed the concept of traditional staff development by advancing the idea of coaching, the practice of ongoing peer support. The results of such collaborative professional development were astonishing. Their research documented that while professional development must provide a strong understanding of theory, other factors, such as demonstration, practice, and most important, peer coaching or collaborative opportunities, were essential for transferring the knowledge to the classroom. They reported significant increases in student learning when participants were provided ongoing support in addition to high-quality professional development that allowed for modeling and practice. This research, in combination with Peter Senge's concepts of learning organizations outlined in his book *The Fifth Discipline*, created a shift in how professional development was delivered. Senge argued that the whole can exceed the sum of its parts. His notion of "systems thinking" advanced the concept that "building shared vision, models, team learning, and personal mastery" is necessary to realize the system's potential (1990, 12). "At the heart of a learning organization is a shift of mind—from seeing ourselves as separate from the world to connected to the world, from seeing problems as caused by someone or something 'out there' to seeing how our own actions create the problems we experience. A learning organization is a place where people are continually discovering how they create their reality. And how they can change it" (12).

Districts all over the nation soon began to think in terms of professional learning communities (PLCs), sometimes referred to as communities of continuous inquiry and improvement, and many schools and districts spend hundreds of thousands of dollars on initiatives that promise increased student achievement by utilizing PLCs. Books abound that offer tips and formulas for PLC success. Educational organizations, such as Southwest Educational Development Laboratory (SEDL) provide comprehensive summaries of the attributes of a successful professional learning community, and many schools have used these attributes to customize their own PLCs. SEDL suggests that professional learning communities should include

◆ the collegial and facilitative participation of the principal, who shares leadership—and thus, power and authority—through inviting staff input in decision making

◆ a shared vision that is developed from staff's unswerving commitment to students' learning and that is consistently articulated and referenced for the staff's work

◆ collective learning among staff and application of that learning to solutions that address students' needs

◆ the visitation and review of each teacher's classroom behavior by peers as a feedback and assistance activity to support individual and community improvement and

◆ physical conditions and collegial relationships that support such an operation (1997, 11)

The success of a learning community lies in its willingness to forge the way itself, fostering elements that create a learning organization: inquiry, intellectual curiosity, dialogue, and respect.

A quick view of the difference between professional learning communities and traditional professional development is provided in Figure 1.1.

## Traditional Professional Development Versus Professional Learning Communities

| Traditional Professional Development | Professional Learning Communities |
|---|---|
| Teachers have little input into content or development, which is often one-size-fits-all workshops. | Staff determines content based on teaching and learning needs specifically related to the school. |
| Learning takes place on inservice days. | Learning is embedded in workday. |
| Instruction occurs in whole group. | Collaboration occurs in small groups. |
| Presenter or expert leads workshops. | Staff members lead meetings. |
| Purpose of the workshop is to provide new knowledge, techniques, or instructional practices. | Purpose of meetings is to promote understanding and learning. |
| Outcomes are defined by short-term knowledge gains. | Outcomes are long-term, sustained, and flexible. |
| Staff remains isolated after session. | Staff collaboration occurs during and after meetings. |
| Assessment of success is validated by those outside school. | Assessment of success is validated by participants. |
| Administrator's role is as leader. | Administrator role is as colearner. |
| The goal is training of teachers. | The goal is inquiry, reflection, and increased teacher and student learning. |
| Follow-up includes checklist of behaviors. | Follow-up includes peer coaching, action research, and study groups. |
| Participants are passive receivers of knowledge. | Participants are active practitioners of knowledge. |
| Goal is individual mastery of skills. | Goal is problem solving through collegiality and collaboration. |

FIGURE 1.1

© 2007 by ReLeah Cossett Lent from *Literacy Learning Communities*. Portsmouth, NH: Heinemann.

Learning is at once deeply personal and inherently social; it connects us not just to knowledge in the abstract, but to each other.

                                —Peter Senge, *Schools That Learn*

Professional learning communities, then, create opportunities for collaborative inquiry and collective wisdom that emerge as teachers, principals, and other staff members work together to apply the newly gained knowledge in authentic and relevant educational settings. As Linda Darling-Hammond notes, "In the new paradigm staff development is a shared, public process; promotes sustained interaction; emphasizes substantive school-related issues; relies on internal expertise; expects teachers to be active participants; emphasizes the why as well as the how of teaching; articulates a theoretical research base; and anticipates that lasting change will be a slow process" (Darling-Hammond and Sykes 1999, 134).

Admittedly, traditional professional development was easier to implement, manage, and assess, especially with the ubiquitous pre- and post-tests. Districts or schools still insistent on realizing such quickly quantifiable advantages, however, risk losing the important, longer-range benefits of community. Dennis Sparks reports on a study by Lee, Smith, and Crominger of 820 secondary schools, in which they "determined that in schools characterized as learning communities, staff members did indeed hold collective responsibility for the learning of students, worked together and changed their teaching. As a result, students had greater academic gains in science, math, history and reading than those in traditionally organized schools. According to the researchers, teachers in these schools also reported more satisfaction in their work, had higher morale, and were absent less often" (Sparks 2002, 6-4).

The Southwest Educational Development Laboratory outlines the following among a longer list of positive results in schools engaging in professional learning communities:

◆ reduced isolation of teachers

◆ collective responsibility for students' success

◆ powerful learning that defines good teaching and classroom practice that creates new knowledge and beliefs about teaching and learners

◆ increased meaning and understanding of the content that teachers teach and the roles they play in helping all students achieve expectations

◆ more satisfaction, higher morale, and lower rates of absenteeism for students and teachers

◆ higher likelihood of undertaking fundamental systemic change

◆ decreased dropout rates for students

◆ smaller achievement gaps between students from different backgrounds. (1997, 5)

While these and other advantages have been observed and documented in schools incorporating professional learning communities, they may not be easily or immediately measured since they occur over time as a natural result of the process. Unfortunately, as anyone who has been in education for even a short time understands, massive federal and state bureaucracies often undermine the very objectives they espouse. The No Child Left Behind (NCLB) Act, for example, has standardized teaching and learning to such an extent that accountability measures must be easily compared, sorted, and filed. The opportunity for collaboration, time for deep reflection, and freedom to experiment with new practices, all necessary components for learning communities, get lost in the accountability shuffle. As such, those in charge of accountability often act as if only that which is assessable is worthy of our time, money, or energy. I prefer to err on the side of Albert Einstein who said, "Not everything that can be counted counts, and not everything that counts can be counted." Imagine those words as a mission statement in schools or districts. Instead, professional development directors often fail to allow time for human elements to take root before they begin counting the beans. Those in the business of creating a product may not agree with Einstein because they are counting in different ways than educators count. Educators count within the fragile hearts, minds, and psyches of human beings, not within an economic system that counts profit.

An ambitious principal in an upscale district pressured by standards-based accountability became frustrated because she had spent all her professional development funds implementing professional learning communities for the purpose of increasing student test scores. The teachers initially were enthusiastic about the approach and organized into communities, anxious to begin the process of professional learning and dialogue. They soon felt the principal's impatience, however, and the resulting anxiety to quantify student learning gains led to a panicked sense that the learning communities were not moving along quickly enough to ensure progress by the testing date. The principal began to insist that the messy business of learning be graphed on neat data charts that reflected only out-comes, not the sometimes circuitous flow of inquiry and reflection. This atmosphere destroyed the slowly developing professional learning commu-nities, in effect relegating this progressive initiative to the more tradi-tional professional development of the past. In this school, professional learning communities became just one more program that required teach-ers to go through the motions, check items off the master list, and fulfill their professional development requirements. The list looked something like this:

**PLC Check-Off List**

◆ Write a mission statement.

◆ Choose an area of focus based upon student data.

◆ Find best practices.

◆ Implement best practices.

◆ Test students and hold breath for adequate yearly progress.

One teacher in this school noted that the staff would have done well to have spent the first year discussing and understanding "PLC terms," such as *mission statement*, *best practices*, and *student data*, before begin-ning the process. The list, while it may have been useful as a structure on which to hang professional learning, was mistaken for the learning itself. Hargreaves points out that staff development frequently falls short of our expectations because it "does not acknowledge or address the personal identities and moral purposes of teachers, nor the cultures and contexts in which they work" (2006, 14).

A professional learning community is a breathing, living, changing process that will not look the same in each school or district, just as any type of community differs according to its individual characteristics. While it is true that we must start with the end—student learning—in mind, we must also begin at the beginning and that means that we must trust each other enough to believe that there are some things that should not be meas-ured, graphed, and assessed. We must believe that relationships, observa-tions, experiences, and motivation play a significant role in our success as teachers and our students' success as learners. Mandating change or growth, much like mandating community, begs for a quick fix that flames initially and then smolders with resentment, frustration, and discourage-ment. Effective professional learning communities grow outward from individuals and circumstances and must be constructed on a solid infra-structure based on the needs of that community.

In offering advice on building professional learning communities, Michael Fullen addresses the human element that is an intrinsic part of the collaborative effort of professional learning. "Fostering professional learning communities should include forums for teachers to collectively reflect on and collaborate on the ethical and moral dimensions of their work and behavior" (2006, 51). He notes that professional learning communities should not be confined to the latest ideas and innovations, but places where "teachers can explore elements of their own practice that they see as ethically responsive or problematic" (51). As in all of his work, Fullen supports the concept of socially based elements of community, such as trust, motivation, inclusion, collaboration, and respect. "All successful turnarounds develop collaboration where there was none before. When relationships develop, trust increases as do other measures of social capital and social cohesion" (54).

Even before professional learning communities became a popular practice in schools, Parker Palmer was advocating their use in his groundbreaking and heartening book *The Courage to Teach*. His notions of community remind us of the fundamental values inherent in teaching and its parallels to learning. Neither are standardized or formulaic, and both involve a human element that cannot be packaged. Few have said it better than he with these words:

> When I imagine the community of truth gathered around some great thing—from DNA to *The Heart of Darkness* to the French Revolution—I wonder: Could teachers gather around the great thing called "teaching and learning" and explore its mysteries with the same respect we accord any subject worth knowing? We need to learn how to do so, for such a gathering is one of the few means we have to become better teachers. There are no formulas for good teaching and the advice of experts has but marginal utility. If we want to grow in our practice, we have two primary places to go: to the inner ground from which good teaching comes and to the community of fellow teachers from whom we can learn more about ourselves and our craft." (1998, 141)

Parker's point, that gathering and exploring is fundamental to a learning community, underscores the importance of remaining above the urgent directives to continually assess its outcome. We must remind each other that the essence of community lies within our collective humanity, and the very qualities that give it life are those that are difficult to quantify, standardize, categorize, or assess. We must agree to value that which refuses to fit into quantifiable molds—ambiguity, dissonance, reflection, and trust—while the results appear in much the same way that Carl Sandberg describes fog, "on little cat feet" sitting on "silent haunches"—a natural and evolutionary outcome of a process that works (1992, 81).

## Questions for Reflection

1. Identify communities that you have been a part of in the past; for example, churches, clubs, sororities or fraternities, music groups, neighborhood, sports.

2. Which characteristics of the community made it strong?

3. Which characteristics were ones that had the potential of undermining its effectiveness?

4. What barriers do you see to forming communities within your school, department, or team?

5. How might each of these barriers be overcome?

## Reflection Through Action

Begin by forming a small community at your school or district with a few people who have a common interest, challenge, or situation. Instead of casually talking in the hall if you happen upon someone who might be a part of this community, set a time and place for an informal gathering either at school or at a place outside of school, such as a restaurant. Once your "community" has met, ask them if they would like to continue to meet on a regular basis to engage in dialogue about students, instructional practices, or your school life in general.

## Study Group Resources: Forming a Community

◆ *The Courage to Teach: Exploring the Inner Landscape of a Teacher's Life* (Palmer 1998)

- ◆ *In Schools We Trust: Creating Communities of Learning in an Era of Testing and Standardization* (Meier 2002)
- ◆ *Professional Development in Learning-Centered Schools* (Caldwell 1997)
- ◆ *Schools That Learn: A Fifth Discipline Fieldbook for Educators, Parents, and Everyone Who Cares About Education* (Senge et al. 2000)

# Why Trust Matters

Our distrust is very expensive.

—RALPH WALDO EMERSON

I once taught in a high school where the principal told me that he had lost trust in me. Since I consider trustworthiness one of my better qualities, a comment such as this would normally have distressed me. Instead, I found the remark to be neither unexpected nor unwelcome under the circumstances. The principal didn't trust me because I disagreed with him—rather vehemently—when he told me to censor the award-winning school newspaper I had sponsored for several years. He didn't trust me because I consulted the editor of the local newspaper for advice when he ordered me to censor. Further, he didn't trust me because I showed my disloyalty when I challenged his decision to restrict the novel *Of Mice and Men* from whole-class instruction because of one parent's complaint.

The last incident says much about the entire culture of trust in that school. It had been an uneventful day when the principal walked into the English workroom where twenty high school English teachers awaited him in this hastily called meeting. He announced briefly and definitively that he had decided the novel *Of Mice and Men* would no longer be available for use in whole-class instruction due to a parent's complaint. Not *one* of the teachers said a word to him, except me. His reply to my comment was that I could talk to him privately in his office if I so chose. For years I pondered why the other English teachers did not object to this act of censorship. Now

I have come to believe that it was a matter of trust. They did not trust their principal enough to be honest about their evaluation of his actions–or even to discuss the subject with him. In fact, they did not trust each other enough to have a dialogue about it in an open forum, such as a department meeting. As I recall, when these teachers did discuss his actions, their conversations took place in individual classrooms with the doors firmly closed. One of the faculty members who spoke to me about the incident approached me in the faculty parking lot, with no danger of being overheard.

On another occasion, this same principal explained to me that he needed people in leadership positions within the school whom he could trust, people with similar views to his. One of those people, he said, was a teacher with whom he had once coached sports. With that admission, I suddenly understood. Trust, in his view, flowed only in one direction– down from the top. He understood the need to trust those who worked (or played) *for* him, but he did not understand the importance of trust flowing in all directions: up, down, and sideways. He didn't see that trust, or the lack of it, permeates an entire school, including faculty relationships with each other as well as with their students.

My principal's lack of trust led to significant consequences for me. He replaced me as sponsor of the school newspaper with someone who had no experience in journalism and made me vacate the classroom I had occupied for many years. Worse, he dismantled a long-standing team-teaching program that a colleague and I had established and which, according to students and parents alike, had been extremely successful. The principal could not have found a more effective way to relay his message to the other 150 or so staff members: "A teacher's most important goal is to ensure that I, as principal, *trust* you–and trust equals agreement and obedience." The complexities of this distrustful relationship can be read in its entirety in *At the Schoolhouse Gate: Lessons in Intellectual Freedom*, a book I coauthored with Gloria Pipkin. Pipkin further examines in sad detail how a lack of trust can destroy schools and disrupt entire communities.

Without a foundation of trust, members of a school are isolated, disenfranchised, fearful, and often intimidated. Maslow's hierarchy of needs explains how people revert to the most basic instincts, safety and security, especially when threatened. Unfortunately, it is in this state where many school faculty members reside day after day. It is difficult, if not impossible, to tap into the potential collaborative energy that emanates from a group of people who have not been afforded the *freedom* to risk. A state of security and trust is referred to as a "growth state" by Maslow (1954), as opposed to a "deficiency state" where security and survival are paramount. It is in the growth state that problem solving and creativity flourish. If the prime motivation of members in any group, however, is to protect their selfhood or their livelihood, they will not engage in the open and honest dialogue that is essential to long-term school improvement. People who are distrustful will not express their doubts about instructional practices or ask hard questions about curriculum and student learning. In fact, it may be difficult for them even to think about such issues.

In this era of high-stakes testing and accountability by the sword, the fear factor is especially prevalent. The constant threat of school takeovers, loss of funding, or public humiliation invites a schoolwide paranoia that infects the school body like a virus. The deep and thoughtful dialogue that accompanies systemic positive change is cut short by a profound lack of trust as teachers are pitted against each other in a contest for higher-achieving students, a larger amount of "prize money" awarded in some states for high test scores, and an obsessive, frenetic race to cross the finish line, marked by the date of testing. The concept of working together to improve all students' learning morphs into an atmosphere where secrets for success are tightly held, especially in states such as Florida, where schools are given grades, A through F, based on criteria from the No Child Left Behind legislation.

Michael Fullan, in his book *Turnaround Leadership*, quotes Rosabeth Moss Kanter as she describes how a chain reaction can occur in schools that have lost confidence: "Communication decreases, criticism and blame increase, respect decreases, isolation increases, focus turns inward, rifts widen and inequities grow, initiative decreases, aspirations diminish and negativity spreads" (2006, 25). Kanter is describing a school that has fallen into a culture of distrust, one that has entered a state of deficiency.

Joyce and Showers (2002) remind us that knowledge translates to classroom practice and increased student learning when peer support is present, often in the form of coaching . The word *coaching* conjures up images of nurturing relationships where mentors support, guide, and encourage. Yet one of the barriers to successful literacy coaching is that many teachers are uncomfortable having a coach observe them in the classroom. Teachers report that they fear the coach will "report back" to the principal. A teacher in one school remarked, "I don't like to have the coach in my room because I'm not sure whose side she is on." This lack of trust contributes to the disintegration of a collaborative system where everyone is on the same side, supporting each other in their common pursuit of student learning. Teachers who work in a deficient model often prefer working alone or beside a colleague with whom they have developed a bond, rather than risk the formation of a relationship that could hurt them. Often, they are reluctant to make themselves vulnerable by admitting they are having problems in the classroom, as if such an admission implies that they are less than perfect. These illusions of perfection matter in a school where each person acts as an independent contractor bidding for advantages such as better schedules, advanced classes, bonus pay, or leadership opportunities. This lack of trust, prevalent in many schools, is especially common in high schools, where relationships are often divided along departmental lines and competition replaces cooperation in a quest for favors bestowed by those higher in the hierarchical power structure.

Trust must infuse all professional development if growth and student learning are the objectives. Even in schools where faculties have been the recipients of high-quality, long-term professional development, teachers must feel safe enough to try new practices and engage in reflective and collaborative dialogue, or the knowledge they gain may remain dormant, sealed in a vacuum of fear.

In her book *Trust Matters: Leadership for Successful Schools*, Megan Tschannen-Moran (2004) examines the concept of trust and its effect on faculties. In attempting to understand the elusive qualities embedded in trust, she has identified five facets central to trust.

◆ Benevolence: caring, support, expressing appreciation, and being fair

◆ Honesty: integrity, telling the truth, keeping promises, being real

◆ Openness: sharing power, decision making, and important information

◆ Reliability: consistency, dependability, diligence

◆ Competence: engaging in problem solving, fostering conflict resolution, and working hard

Conversely, Tschannen-Moran defines a "Culture of Control" where a proliferation of rules replaces trust. Rules that are top-down and intended to enforce compliance send a clear message that those to whom the rules apply cannot be trusted to do the right thing. This lack of flexibility creates resistance and resentment rather than cooperation and collaboration. Such a control mentality demands blind obedience and blocks innovation and true reform (2004, 101).

In short, trust is not a nicety like some amenity in an upscale hotel. It is essential to school improvement and to student learning. Michael Fullan notes that in schools where trust is promoted, people are more likely to become motivated, which then allows change to occur. Tschannen-Moran documents that in schools where teachers trust each other, they have a greater sense of collaboration, higher morale, and increased efficacy (2004, 124). Teachers in trust-infused schools are more likely to be enthusiastic and organized, as well as devoting more time to planning. Interestingly, teachers who gain self-efficacy, the belief that one can make a difference, are less likely to become angry, impatient, or frustrated with students. Tschannen-Moran notes, "Teachers' sense of efficacy exerts significant influence on student achievement by promoting teacher behaviors that enhance learning. Indeed, high teacher efficacy has been shown to be positively related to higher student achievement" (128).

There is no secret formula for creating trust in a school. Trust, by its very nature, is a process that develops from sustained relationships where one gains confidence in another based on many of the intangible qualities outlined by Tschannen-Moran. When attempting to come to a common understanding of trust, people often use concept-dense words that have layers of meaning, such as *fairness*, *truth*, and *integrity*. Thus, trust cannot be written into official policies, school improvement plans, or professional development blueprints. Its subtleties flourish in an atmosphere, not a document, where relationships are valued and mutual respect is nonnegotiable. Forming trust involves creating a culture of positive expectations and then allowing human beings the time and space they need to learn how to rely on one another for support.

## *The Role of the Principal*

> It is more difficult to build leadership capacity among colleagues than to tell colleagues what to do. It is more difficult to be full partners with other adults engaged in hard work than to evaluate and supervise subordinates.
>
> —Linda Lambert, *Building Leadership Capacity for Lasting School Improvement*

There is absolutely no doubt that the role of the principal is crucial in providing and sustaining a culture of trust. Without such "sustainable leadership," as coined by Hargraeves and Fink in a book by the same title, schoolwide positive change is extremely difficult. In fact, in a recent article titled "Students' Academic Success Can Be a Matter of Principal" from the *Sydney Morning Herald*, reporter Anna Patty (2006) cited research showing that principals who acted as educational leaders, those not "bogged down in management and administrative tasks," were as important as a good teacher in getting results. "Good principals were identified as those who were open to change, were informed risk takers, and were friendly and approachable. Their leadership was highly influential in the development of a positive school culture."

The Southwest Educational Development Laboratory also cited "supported and shared leadership" as an attribute in effective professional learning communities. They succinctly defined the type of leadership necessary for change, as outlined by Lucianne Carmichael, the first resident principal of the Harvard University Principal Center. "The traditional pattern that teachers teach, students learn, and administrators manage is completely altered. There is no longer a hierarchy of who knows more than someone else, but rather the need for everyone to contribute" (1997, 2). Eaker, DuFour, and DuFour differentiate the roles of principals in traditional schools and those in professional learning communities. "In traditional schools, administrators are viewed as being in leadership positions while teachers are viewed as 'implementers' or followers. In professional learning communities, administrators are viewed as leaders of leaders" (2002, 22).

Linda Lambert explains that principals must develop a shared vision by allowing staff and community to "reflect upon their own cherished values, listen to those held by others and make sense through dialogue of how to bring personal and community values together" (2003, 26). While a study on the importance of principal leadership is beyond the scope of this book, it is obviously an essential element in any movement involving systemic change. Principals must be committed to building a school where trust is its centerpiece; otherwise, all the school-reform initiatives in the world will ring hollow and false to those whose primary goal is protecting their individual interests.

Although a school dedicated to systemic, widespread literacy improvement must have a principal committed to its formation, small groups of teachers can make a significant difference in their daily workings by consciously fostering an environment of trust and community. In fact, their endeavors may well be the impetus that blends the colors of their school into a mural of trust. By keeping three elements at the forefront of all professional development, whether in formal whole-faculty settings or in informal private exchanges, individuals can count on Margaret Mead's advice: "Never doubt that a small group of thoughtful, committed citizens can change the world." The three elements? Relationships, dialogue, and respect.

Just as relationship trumps virtually every other element in a successful classroom, relationship at the faculty level is essential for systemic change. By knowing each other and valuing what each person can bring to the school, a faculty marshals its strengths to create a whole that is infinitely smarter, stronger, and more creative than the most talented teachers working in isolation. Such collaboration not only benefits the team collectively but also dramatically affects individuals in the team. The trust that develops through both professional and social interactions creates a type of synergistic intelligence that is satisfying and motivating. This type of bonding does not happen, however, because members are placed together in a room and then dubbed a professional learning community. Faculty members must know each other in order to learn *how* to form such trusting relationships.

## How to Form a Culture of Relationship

◆ Build opportunities into the school day for teamwork by providing structures that encourage coteaching, peer coaching, and professional dialogue. Collaborative teaching/learning opportunities should drive the master schedule.

◆ Allow time during meetings to share stories of success and challenges, both personally and professionally.

◆ Encourage teachers to combine classes for related activities, such as service-learning projects, writing workshops, field trips, or content-area projects.

◆ Make time for small faculty teams to meet for professional study and meaningful, relevant, authentic school-related work based on their interests and their students' needs.

◆ Encourage faculty teams or partners to sponsor clubs, sports, or extracurricular duties.

◆ Plan out-of-school social functions for faculty at sporting events, concerts, community gatherings, or restaurants where entire families are invited.

◆ Create a blog for online discussions or a website where announcements for social outings or study group meetings are featured. Allow space for photographs and family news.

◆ Place name cards at faculty meetings to create different seating arrangements that encourage the staff to interact with those outside their traditional circle of colleagues.

◆ Ask faculty members to identify their strengths, and allow them to have autonomy when possible as they select duties, classes, or extracurricular activities.

◆ Offer multiple intelligence and learning-style tests to faculty during preservice so they better understand themselves as well as their colleagues. Group faculty members into teams according to their intelligences and aptitudes, allowing them time to talk about their common interests and challenges.

◆ Have faculty members fill out a Faculty Interest Inventory such as the one in Figure 2.1, at the beginning of each school year. The results of the surveys should be available to all staff as a way of encouraging them to rely on each other as resources for expanding and deepening their curriculum.

## Faculty Interest Inventory

1. What subjects/grade levels have you taught?
2. What experiences or jobs have you had that you would be willing to share with students as a part of their ongoing learning?
3. What hobbies, skills, or talents do you have that you would be willing to share with the school community?
4. What is your favorite book? Movie?
5. Where is the most interesting place (or places) you have visited or lived?
6. Do you know someone who would be willing to offer his or her expertise in a classroom?
7. What topic or unit within your discipline do you feel you teach best?
8. What innovative ideas for your content area would you be willing to share with others?
9. List the extracurricular areas you might like to sponsor.
10. If money were no object, what would your ideal classroom look like?

FIGURE 2.1

Trust is fostered by understanding each other, even when disagreeing. By talking through issues, reflecting on challenges and successes, and developing unity through shared ideas, trust takes root and grows. When a growth culture exists, collective thinking takes on a life of its own and ignites creativity that can often lead to unprecedented successes and innovative solutions to problems.

## Creating Opportunities for Dialogue

◆ Show the school board or superintendent the importance of professional learning communities by providing research that demonstrates its positive effect on student achievement. Ask for additional planning time for the faculty to engage in study groups that focus on a wide variety of topics related to student learning needs, such as behavior management, adolescent reading, differentiated learning, or writing across the curriculum. Create a plan for sharing the results of such professional learning with other schools in the district or at state and national conferences. See Chapter 7 for more information about this topic.

◆ Restructure faculty meetings so they become working sessions that deepen thinking as well as relationships. Housekeeping items can be handled through emails or announcements. Whenever possible, every faculty, team, or department meeting should involve a discussion on an educational topic or student learning need. Dialogue may be prompted by providing an article from a professional journal such as *Educational Leadership* or the *Journal of Staff Development.*

◆ Develop the practice of having teachers videotape each other teaching or their students learning. Use the tapes for sharing instructional practices, engaging in peer coaching, or self-reflection.

◆ Have the faculty develop a department and/or schoolwide statement about what is most important for the school and their students. This statement is not necessarily one that will appear on school stationary or be posted above the welcome desk at the front office. It will, instead, reflect the deeply held beliefs of the school community. Ask students to contribute to the thinking.

◆ Provide schoolwide professional development on coaching. Emphasize the objective, nonjudgmental actions and attitudes of good coaches.

Encourage teachers periodically to observe each other – not for evaluative purposes – but to learn from each other. See Chapter 8 for more information about this topic.

◆ Begin faculty or department meetings with prompts like those in
Figure 2.2 as a way of encouraging staff members to reflect on their
teaching/learning through writing or discussion.

## Building a Culture of Respect: Focusing on Growth

I once visited an inner-city high school and saw students picking up trash
at lunch and cleaning off their tables in the open courtyard. When the bell
rang to signal students' return to class, the courtyard was litter free. As I
looked around, I realized that the walls were clean and the bathroom mir-
rors were free of the teenage messages that are undeniably a part of student literacy. I asked the principal how he managed to get the students to

---

## Questions to Prompt Dialogue and Writing

1. Describe something that happened recently or share a comment from a student or parent that confirms your decision to become a teacher.
2. Describe one of the most challenging aspects of your teaching life.
3. Describe an interaction or event that took place recently that deserves further reflection.
4. What is the most important issue for our faculty? Our school? Our students?
5. How does your assessment inform instruction? What is the difference between data-driven instruction and data-informed instruction?
6. What urgent challenges do we have, such as bullying, that require our immediate attention?
7. What is the most important thing you do each day?
8. What is least important thing you do each day?
9. What do you enjoy most about your job?
10. What is something new you tried that you weren't sure would be successful?

---

FIGURE 2.2
Adapted from Lent, R. 2006. "Creating a Culture for Writers." *Journal of Staff Development* 27 (3): 47–50.

treat the school in such a respectful way. I will never forget his response: "It's their school. They want to keep it clean." I had a million other questions. "How do you inspire them to *want* to keep it clean? Why do they care? Do all of the students feel this way about their school? What are the consequences for not keeping it clean?" I didn't get specific answers to my questions, but I did come to understand that this culture had not been created in a day or as the result of an order from the principal. The environment of respect that I observed had developed from an attitude of inclusion, a strong commitment to each individual in the school community, and a transfer of ownership from those who run the school to those who inhabit it.

## How to Build a Culture of Respect

◆ Articulate the importance of sustaining a culture of respect and trust by having the staff create ground rules for meetings that include not making negative remarks about students. Post them as a visual reminder of the importance of constructive comments about students and peers.

◆ Encourage a sense of ownership by allowing faculty members and students to create murals on walls related to content-area studies, displays of class projects, and message boards highlighting academic interests, such as a What We're Reading Now board.

◆ Ensure that *all* voices are heard and valued in meetings, and remind each other that the most important thing we can do is listen to each other.

◆ Resist the impulse to create a hierarchy of leadership. Encourage shared or rotated leadership responsibilities, with the leader always acting as a facilitator.

◆ Create an environment where teachers feel safe to question the status quo.

◆ Help the staff view professional disagreement and cognitive dissonance as necessary elements of the growth process. Ensure that those who have differences are heard and not discounted or slighted because they dare to disagree. Develop a method for dealing with disputes.

◆ Consider returning any money given by the state as a "reward" for high test scores. Remind each other that trust and community are more valuable than money, especially since many faculties that have accepted bonuses for test scores report a disintegration of trust and unity when having to make decisions about who gets what slice of the bonus pie.

◆ Make sure that the staff and students know that diversity of thought and experience is an asset, not a liability.

◆ Objectively assess progress midyear and at the end of the school year, acknowledging every individual who contributed to growth, innovation, or collaborative learning.

◆ View problems as challenges, not barriers, and address them by tapping into the skills and talents of faculty members and students.

◆ Provide comp time, stipends, or other benefits to teachers who give their own time for professional learning. Make a statement that the work teachers do related to professional growth is important and valued by offering opportunities for teachers to attend and present at conferences and district workshops.

◆ If your budget allows, plan retreats away from school for extended study and dialogue. Such activities will also encourage and deepen faculty bonds.

◆ Make all meetings open to all members of the faculty. Secret meeting or meetings by invitation create distrust and divisiveness.

Why does trust matter? Because relationships matter, especially in the business of schooling. Our work touches that most elusive part of the human spirit, and our greatest rewards often appear as intangible flickers of learning that cross the faces of those in our classrooms each day. When a faculty creates a culture of trust, it immerses all its members, including students, in an environment where relationships have the potential of turning knowledge into wisdom.

## Questions for Reflection

1. In your personal life, who do you trust?

2. What characteristics does this person possess that makes him or her worthy of your trust?

3. To what extent do you trust other people in your school, such as colleagues, administrators, students?

4. How important is trust in your own relationships?

5. What factors diminish trust?

## *Reflection Through Action*

Encourage dialogue related to trust by engaging your department (or the entire faculty) in an analysis of the "trust factor" within the school. Address each component of Tschannen-Moran's five facets of trust by recording on a large sheet of paper the group's comments, perhaps using a chart like the one in Figure 2.3. Take enough time to discuss the complex meaning of each facet and find examples within the school.

The purpose of this exercise is to define trust and consider to what extent it exists in the school community at large. Remind groups that the chart is merely a tool for prompting conversations; it is not the means to an end. As such, the faculty may wish to add other facets of trust in addition to the five identified by Tschannen-Moran. Note that participants initially may feel uncomfortable discussing such concepts because faculty discussions rarely go beyond the superficial language required for straightforward decision making. If a school is committed to forming professional learning communities, however, it must begin by delving deeply into attitudes, actions, and feelings by using language to foster respect and positive action instead of cultivating complaints and discouragement.

## *Study Group Resources: Building Trust*

- *The Moral Imperative of School Leadership* (Fullan 2003)
- *Strengthening the Heartbeat: Leading and Learning Together in Schools* (Sergiovanni 2004)
- *Trust Matters: Leadership for Successful Schools* (Tschannen-Moran 2004)

| Facets of Trust | Definition as it applies to our school | Examples in our school | Challenges to its formation | Actions that will encourage it | Comments |
|---|---|---|---|---|---|
| Benevolence | | | | | |
| Honesty | | | | | |
| Openness | | | | | |
| Reliability | | | | | |
| Competence | | | | | |

FIGURE 2.3 *Facets of Trust Dialogue Chart*

© 2007 by ReLeah Cossett Lent from *Literacy Learning Communities*. Portsmouth, NH: Heinemann.

# Why Literacy Learning Matters

The many books he read but served to whet his unrest. Every page of every book was a peep-hole into the realm of knowledge. His hunger fed upon what he read, and increased.

—JACK LONDON, *MARTIN EDEN* (1909)

It was one of those days that I love. In my role as consultant, my task was to visit classes, talk with students, and observe teachers as I gathered informal data that I could use to support my work in this particular high school. The first classroom I walked into looked like one where real learning was taking place. Students in groups of three or four had pulled their desks together and there was a quiet buzz of voices. The teacher was engaging one group in a discussion while the other groups appeared to be involved in some type of assignment.

I pulled up a chair and joined a trio of two girls and a boy. They shuffled their books nervously at my approach and assumed the position of students who might appear in a Norman Rockwell setting, although I thought the pierced nose of one of the girls enhanced the effect. "What are you doing?" I asked, trying for a tone that was more conversational than evaluative.

"Answering questions," replied one of the girls.

"Where do the questions come from?" I asked.

"The back of the chapter," one of them responded.

"Do you have to read the entire chapter to answer the questions?" I wondered aloud.

"No—you can just go back through the chapter and look for the answers," the other girl said.

"Do you talk with each other about the questions and answers?" I asked.

All three glanced at me, presumably to find out if the question was for real.

"Uh . . . sometimes," the boy responded, clearly uncomfortable with my many questions.

"I'm trying to find out about high school students' reading and learning habits. Do you mind talking to me for a few minutes?" I said, realizing I should have started with this introduction.

They made eye contact with me now that they had determined I wasn't trying to trap them into some type of admission that could be used against them later. "Okay," one of the girls responded as the other nodded her head. The boy still didn't look convinced.

"What I want to know is how much reading is required for this class—actually for all of your classes."

"We don't have to read much at all," they all agreed.

"Then how do you pass?" I asked.

Although they struggled a bit with explaining that they were bright enough and had had enough experience to be able to find the answers to questions in the text, they had no trouble at all telling me they did as little as possible to get by. They took notes from lectures, studied their notes (if they had time) before tests, and turned in the answers to the questions at the end of every chapter. It was a simple procedure that had worked for them in most classes, except one, they noted, where the teacher provided a supplemental reading list of fiction and nonfiction books on topics they were studying in history. "It's a hard class, but she's an awesome teacher," one of the girls offered.

"What makes her awesome?" I asked, intrigued.

"Well, she makes class really interesting by bringing in all kinds of stories and facts. We have great discussions, and she lets us read other stuff besides the textbook. We do projects in groups."

"You could have a discussion among yourselves right now as you answer these questions. Maybe that would make this assignment more interesting," I suggested. I gathered from their expressions that they didn't think this was a great idea. "Well, why not?" I pressed.

"Because all we have to do is answer the questions," the boy responded.

I decided to get right to the point. "Is it possible to pass this class without even thinking?"

"I don't know," replied one of the girls. "Thinking about *what?*"

These were only three of many students I talked with that day, but I will always remember them, heads close together as they fanned the pages of their books seeking answers to questions that had little or no meaning to them. The other students I visited confirmed the sad sense that I was witnessing a type of pseudolearning. Students did what they had to do to pass a class but for the most part they were disengaged in learning. A shining exception was a class where students were working in groups at computers creating architectural models. They showed me their portfolios and explained how their collaborative work would eventually come together to create some rather amazing structures. I didn't understand all their drawings and computer images, but I was disappointed when it was time to move on to another class.

The teachers in this school were caring, knowledgeable professionals, but in too many cases they had been unable to help their students become responsible for their own learning. Even their most able students admitted that they were playing the schooling game rather than being intrinsically involved in learning. When I reported my student conversations to the literacy team, however, teachers responded that they were doing their best to engage their students by introducing reading strategies and even allowing kids to work in groups as suggested by educational research. Deeper conversations unveiled a disturbing, fatalistic attitude on the part of some the faculty. "If I had it to do over, I wouldn't have become a teacher," a social studies teacher reported. "I love working with kids, but I'm not sure I'm giving them what they need, and the demands are increasing to make sure they achieve. I have more and more material to cover and the kids *will not* read their textbooks. The truth is I can't make them read, and if I penalize them for not reading, they will either fail the class or drop out. It's a no-win situation."

In fact, his students are not unlike millions of others across the United States, many of whom are dropping out—in record numbers—and teachers are feeling pressured to keep them in school at any cost. Why are students so disengaged? There is no one answer to this complex question, of course, but I often wonder if we are asking our students to learn in ways that are in such contrast to their realities that only the most persistent are able to produce what we expect from them. An article in *Time* magazine titled "How to Bring Our Schools Out of the 20th Century," begins with a joke about how Rip Van Winkle awakened in the twenty-first century, bewildered and frightened at all of the things he sees, such as cell phones, video games, transportation, and shopping malls. He is only reassured when he enters a classroom because he recognizes everything as it was when he went to sleep a hundred years earlier (Wallis and Steptoe 2006). Perhaps this joke is not so funny. Are we requiring twenty-first-century students to learn in the same way twentieth-century students learned? If so, it is no surprise that we, as educators, are becoming as frustrated and discouraged as our students.

CBS News reported on education in 2006 by asking, "Will High Schools Be a Relic of the Past?" They interviewed North Carolina's governor, who had implemented a new program called Early Colleges to confront the state's high dropout rate. He had relocated some of the state's high schools on college campuses where students could obtain both a high school diploma and a two-year associate's degree by the time they turned eighteen. Stories such as this force us to address why literacy learning matters. At the risk of sounding alarmist, I will argue that it is not enough to go through a menu of reading strategies in the hope that one or more will become the elixir that suddenly turns students into a generation of literate readers, writers, and thinkers who will prove their worth on standardized tests and allow us to use their adequate yearly progress as notches on our belts. If secondary schools are not to become, as CBS reported, "a quaint relic of the past," we must come to understand our students where they *are*, not where we think they are; examine current literacy research; and connect the two in ways that make our schools places where today's students choose to stay.

## Today's Literacies

> A myth that supports all of the effort to drill into children things they do not understand is that learning has to precede understanding.
>
> —FRANK SMITH, *INSULT TO INTELLIGENCE*

Despite the National Reading Panel's report that attempted to define reading with five components (phonemic awareness, phonics, fluency, vocabulary, and comprehension), it takes only a few minutes of being with adolescents to see that, in many cases, they are employing reading and literacy skills that go far beyond those elements. They email, use instant messaging, communicate in blogs, and create entire Web spaces that reflect their own literacies. They download music, write poetry, and read young adult literature and e-books about such varied topics as vampires, space travel, and relationships. They play video games that require an impressive amount of critical thinking and decision making, and demonstrate shared literacy, teamwork, and effective social skills as they communicate with peers who may live on a different continent and speak a different language. They discuss with piercing insight important issues such as school shootings and read long nonfiction articles related to their lives or their interests. Dubbed Generation M, for Multitaskers, this generation is also adept at digital literacy, which entails parallel processing, instant decision making, and adapting to simultaneous noise, images, and collaboration. The new iPhone—a phone, iPod, and mini-Internet computer all rolled into one—isn't even considered revolutionary to this generation. Our students may not look literate as they sit in groups and skim chapters in textbooks looking for correct answers to someone else's questions, but they are incredibly literate in ways that count for them and for our society.

What is literacy learning and how has literacy changed in the past several years? David Warlick, author of *Redefining Literacy for the 21st Century*, suggests that educators must redefine literacy if we hope to prepare our students for a future that we cannot even describe. "The very nature of information is changing: how you find it, what it looks like, the way it behaves, where it comes from, what you can do with it, and how we, as authors, create it" (2004, x). He contends that we are working in schools where many libraries were "built before the advent of the personal computer—during the Industrial Age" (x). Schools cannot continue to implement traditional curriculum about literacy when it has morphed into something we don't understand or in some cases fully recognize. To pretend that literacy is a one-dimensional activity to be used for school-related purposes—whether to answer questions in a textbook or pass a test for graduation—is to fail our literacy-savvy students before we even begin the complex task of teaching and learning.

Understanding the literacy lives of our students requires understanding our students' literacy habits. Often, we jump into instruction without first determining students' strengths, needs, and the context for learning. A survey such as the one in Figure 3.1 is a starting point for finding and using relevant data about students' literacy learning before creating any type of workable plan. Faculty members should complete the survey as well and compare their answers to students' answers as a measure of how the literacies of each group are similar and different.

# What Is Your Literacy Quotient?

1. What is the best book you have ever read?
   - Did you read it in class or on your own?
2. What types of books do you like to read? (Circle all that apply.)

   **Fiction**

   | | | | | |
   |---|---|---|---|---|
   | Romance | Historical | Science fiction | Fantasy | Sports |
   | Teen drama | Supernatural | Adventure | Serial books | Short stories |
   | Graphic novels | Horror | Poetry | Realistic | Humorous |

   Other _____

   **Nonfiction**

   | | | | |
   |---|---|---|---|
   | Biography | Sports | True-life adventure | Almanacs |
   | Books of facts or lists | | Books about a hobby | Science |

   Other _____

3. What magazines do you like to read?
4. Do you regularly read the newspaper?
   - If so, what sections do you like to read?
   - If so, do you read online or in print format?
5. How do you use the Internet?
6. Do you like to write?
   - If so, what do you write? (include all forms of written communication, such as instant messaging or blogging).
7. What types of videos and movies do you watch?
8. What types of music do you enjoy?
9. How do you use technology? (Circle all that apply.)

   | | | |
   |---|---|---|
   | Instant messaging | Blogging | GPS |
   | Online video games | E-books | Email |
   | Text messaging | Bluetooth | DVD/CD |
   | Personal computer | Pocket PC | Wi-Fi |
   | Video websites (Ex: YouTube) | Personal Websites (Ex: MySpace) | |
   | MP3 player (Ex: iPod) | Digital video recorder (Ex: Tivo) | |

10. Literacy used to mean only the ability to read and write. What does literacy mean for students today?
11. How can your teachers help you become more literate so that you will succeed in school and in life?
12. What challenges do you face with reading, writing, communicating, or using technology?

FIGURE 3.1

We're drowning in information and starving for knowledge.

—RUTHERFORD D. ROGERS, AMERICAN LIBRARIAN

Our students have been born into a society where information is the ruling aristocracy and knowledge is capital. As such, the key to individual and organizational success in the future will be accorded to those who not only have the ability to read, write, and communicate effectively, but also have the ability to learn instead of memorizing and reciting isolated bits of information. In such a learning society, communication and teaming will be marketable assets. Those who thrive in this society must be able to locate and access information, process it, and apply it appropriately. Such skills require deep and critical thinking related to multiple literacies, the type of thinking that students are engaging in on their own today.

Our task, then, goes far beyond effectively employing literacy quick fixes that are offered to us in professional development settings. We must reenvision our roles in this three-dimensional literacy world to be co-learners with students, and such reenvisioning requires understanding, dialogue, teamwork, and patience. Andy Hargreaves, in his book *Teaching in the Knowledge Society*, explains: "Teaching beyond the knowledge economy entails developing the values and emotions of young people's character; emphasizing emotional as well as cognitive learning; building commitments to group life and not just short-term teamwork; and cultivating a cosmopolitan identity which shows genuine curiosity towards and willingness to learn from other cultures, and develop responsibility towards excluded groups within and beyond one's own society" (1994, 4). Such teaching, Hargraeves contends, means committing to formal professional learning and working with colleagues in long-term settings. We all have much to understand if we hope to support our students' transitions from our generation to their own.

Our own learning, then, as educators of twenty-first–century students, matters more now than ever in the past. We cannot rely solely on literacy strategies to support literacy learning, no matter how much they initially have helped us unlock the cognitive processes involved in reading. We could spend millions of dollars playing spin the bottle with attractive literacy initiatives, especially with the hundreds of packaged curriculum options available. Even if we use strategies appropriately, we still must decide which ones to use, and when, and with whom—and how. Our decisions must be informed and customized to the needs of our students, and those needs change from year to year, student to student. With all the factors involved in literacy learning, from multiple literacies to preparing students for a knowledge society and helping them access and apply information, schools cannot survive without examining literacy in the twenty-first century and forming a plan for professional learning to take us safely and expeditiously to the heart of student learning.

Effective literacy learning communities will begin by asking questions and seeking understanding in their quest for answers. They will broaden the definitions of literacy as they make the shift from covering vast quantities of content in departmentalized, isolated units of study to a type of learning that uses knowledge as a conduit to understanding. This new concept of literacy will focus on *engaging* learners in ways that allow them to interact with information rather than being passive recipients of it. Such a new literacy may include what Ron Ritchhart (2002), in his book *Intellectual Character,* calls "an integrated approach" that incorporates characteristics such as those described in a policy document created by the Association for the Advancement of Science, *Project 2061: Science for All Americans.* The project authors identified the following seven "habits of mind" in order to provide a national direction for science curricula.

◆ Integrity

◆ Diligence

◆ Fairness

◆ Curiosity

◆ Openness to new ideas

◆ Skepticism

◆ Imagination

How do such characteristics relate to literacy? Figure 3.2 explains how characteristics such as the ones listed above are necessary for literacy learning.

Ritchhart (2002) reports that one school used these characteristics to develop Five Habits of Mind and ask questions that inform instruction and curriculum. In *Engaging Adolescent Learners: A Guide for Content-Area Teachers* (Lent 2006), I suggest that such questions become an intrinsic part of learning in every subject area so that students practice *how* to learn, not *what* to learn.

# Characteristics of Twenty-first–Century Literacy Learning

| Project 2061 Characteristics | Relates to Twenty-first–Century Literacy Learning |
|---|---|
| Integrity | Learners will recognize that truthfulness and reliability are an integral part of literacy. They will learn to evaluate the integrity of literacy sources and the accuracy of new information. |
| Diligence | Learners will recognize that persistence and determination are necessary for in-depth understanding of multiple literacies, especially as they begin to apply what they learn. |
| Fairness | Learners will consider fairness and equality in their communication with others and in their roles as informed citizens, workers, and lifelong learners. |
| Curiosity | Learners will come to understand and value the process of inquiry to gain deeper understanding and solve problems. |
| Openness to New Ideas | Learners will learn to dialogue with others and consider new ideas by becoming open to possibilities beyond what is presented to them in a single source or format. |
| Skepticism | Learners will question and think critically about what is communicated to them through various literacies. |
| Imagination | Learners will visualize, create, and make connections as they move beyond text or media to adapt learning to new situations. |

FIGURE 3.2

© 2007 by ReLeah Cossett Lent from *Literacy Learning Communities*. Portsmouth, NH: Heinemann.

1.  Evidence: How do we know?

2.  Viewpoint: Who's speaking?

3.  Connections: What causes what?

4.  Supposition: How might things be different?

5.  Meaningfulness: What's the point? Why does it matter?

Imagine a school that focuses on such questions to tap into deep, meaningful learning. Imagine a faculty that unleashes its collective wisdom to explore literacy issues unique to its school. Imagine a schoolwide learning community where students, parents, and community members learn along with faculty about literacy and then make informed choices about how they can meet their students' individualized needs.

## Learning: For Students and Adults

> The principles of learning and their implications for designing learning environments apply equally to child and adult learning.
>
> —NATIONAL RESEARCH COUNCIL, *HOW PEOPLE LEARN:*
> *BRAIN, MIND, EXPERIENCE AND SCHOOL*

Just as we must understand literacy if we are to become a community of literacy learners, we must understand the nature of learning. The past several decades have yielded a vast amount of information about the human brain and unprecedented knowledge about how we learn. For example, Brian Cambourne (1995), head of the Centre for Studies in Literacy at Wollongong University in Australia, has researched the conditions for learning for more than twenty years. His theories have been used successfully by thousands of teachers in schools in Australia, New Zealand, the United States, and Canada. We now know that certain conditions are essential for engagement and deep understanding—both necessary elements for literacy learning.

### Cambourne's Conditions for Learning

◆   *Immersion* Learners are "saturated by, enveloped in, flooded by, steeped in, or constantly bathed in that which is to be learned." They must be immersed in all types of experiences that allow them opportunities for reading, writing, speaking, and listening.

- *Demonstration*  Learners "observe (see, hear, witness, experience, feel, study, explore) actions and artifacts." They must have many demonstrations and models of desired behaviors that allow opportunities for students to observe and later attempt learning.

- *Expectations*  Learners receive messages from the one who is providing the learning experience. Expectations are "subtle and powerful coercers of behavior." The learner must hold expectations for himself that he can and will succeed, but teachers must also hold high, realistic expectations for the learner.

- *Responsibility*  Learners are "permitted to make some decisions (i.e., take responsibility) about what they'll engage with and what they'll ignore." Factors such as when, what, and how regarding the learning are a part of the decision-making process. The teacher must show the learner how to acquire and maintain responsibility.

- *Approximation*  Learners approximate learning or, as Cambourne says, "have a go at it." They are not expected to have mastered the learning, and there should be no anxiety associated with the experimentation. Learners must feel safe to take risks and make mistakes. They need to know that their attempts at learning are vital and important steps in the process. Mistakes are essential for learning to occur.

- *Use*  Learners must have ample opportunities for using and practicing the new learning. They must learn how to apply concepts and take control over learning. This must take place in relevant settings while doing authentic tasks.

- *Response*  Learners must have appropriate feedback from knowledgeable others. Responses should be "relevant, appropriate, timely, readily available, and nonthreatening, with no strings attached" (1995, 185-87).

Figure 3.3 shows a graphic that depicts Cambourne's Conditions of Learning as they occur simultaneously, rather than linearly.

The National Research Council's groundbreaking book titled *How People Learn: Brain, Mind, Experience, and School* proposes a framework designed for "environments that can optimize learning." These include the following:

1. Schools and classrooms must be learner centered.

2. Attention must be given to what is taught, why it is taught, and what competence looks like.

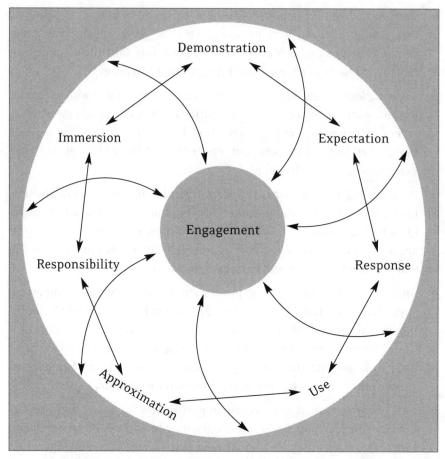

FIGURE 3.3 *Brian Cambourne's Conditions of Learning*

3. Formative assessments – ongoing assessments designed to make students' thinking visible to both teachers and students – are essential.

4. Learning is influenced in fundamental ways by the context in which it takes place. A community center approach requires the development of norms for the classroom and school, as well as connections to the outside world, that support core learning values (2000, 23-26).

The National Research Council makes an essential point that often has been overlooked when schools are embarking upon professional development. Just as conditions for learning are essential for students, they are also critical for adults. The council notes that professional development in the past frequently has been not learner centered, not knowledge centered, not assessment centered, and not community centered. It is little wonder that inservice has so often been unproductive and that the knowledge teachers gained in isolated settings has not transferred to student learning. Unfortunately, districts and administrators have spent so much time frantically responding to the overwhelming NCLB mandates that they haven't been given the time to allow teachers to engage in the slow, deliberate process of learning. By ignoring the basic tenets of learning and the environment in which it must take place, we are not optimizing our own learning potential as adults and, worse, shortchanging students who are depending on us to help them meet the diverse literacies that await them upon graduation.

Not only must we assist students in seeking and constructing meaning, but we, as their teachers and mentors, must also attend to our own learning. It is the only way to address, as Hargreaves says, "our greatest hunger," which is the "quest to know, to understand, to communicate, and to leave the world a better place" (2006, 33).

## Questions for Reflection

*GREAT!*

1. What does it mean to learn?

2. What has been your greatest learning experience? What made it so?

3. What resources help you become a more thoughtful learner?

4. What type of learner are you? How do you learn best?

5. What do you learn from your students?

## Reflection Through Action

In groups, explore the concept of learning by engaging in a dialogue centered on the following questions. Then, create a statement that expresses your group's understanding of learning.

1. Describe a learning experience that was difficult for you.

2. To what degree were you successful with this learning experience?

3. Refer back to Cambourne's Conditions of Learning in this chapter.

   ◆ Which conditions were present in your learning?

   ◆ Which were missing?

◆ How would the learning experience have been different if the conditions were present?

4. Describe a successful learning experience you have had with students. What made it so?

5. As a group, define learning and post the definition in a prominent place. Ask other groups and students to comment on your definition, altering it as dialogue deepens and new understandings of learning occur.

## Study Group Resources: The Process of Learning

◆ *The Art of Changing the Brain: Enriching the Practice of Teaching by Exploring the Biology of Learning* (Zull 2002)

◆ *Brain Matters: Translating Research into Classroom Practice* (Wolfe 2001)

◆ *Enriching the Brain: How to Maximize Every Learner's Potential* (Jensen 2006)

◆ *How People Learn: Brain, Mind, Experience, and School* (National Research Council 2000)

◆ *The Book of Learning and Forgetting* (Smith 1998)

## Section Two

# *Building a Community for Literacy Learning*

The students continued to write and began to
forge stronger identities and to create a sense
of community and an outlet for expression.

—ERIN GRUWELL, *THE FREEDOM WRITERS DIARY*

The time spent to prepare the school's soil for the plant-
ing of perennial learning communities is worth every
minute. It will take deep roots to support the various
literacy initiatives that emerge as the school transitions
from thickets of isolated groups into a collective, systemic
learning organization. The work during this phase of growth
will be specific yet customized to the school as the initial LLC
assesses the school's literacy learning needs and develops a
plan of action that will be a model for other learning communities that will thrive within this nurturing environment.

A three-year plan will support the growth of schoolwide
literacy learning communities.

◆ Year 1 *Authentic* literacy learning begins with the creation of an initial literacy learning community that will
assess students' literacy learning needs and develop a
plan for meeting those needs.

◆ **Year 2** *Embedded* literacy learning will develop as schoolwide learning communities spawn from the initial LLC and begin to use learning tools such as study groups, peer coaching, and action research.

◆ **Year 3** *Sustained* literacy learning will become the foundation of all school initiatives as the principles of learning are firmly established and employed by both students and faculty.

# Creating a Literacy Learning Community

There is no royal road to learning.

—ENGLISH PROVERB

During my years in the classroom, the first day of a new semester was riddled with anxiety yet bursting with hope. There was no way to predict what experience awaited me with each unique and often random group of students assigned to my English class. While at times absolute magic manifested itself, other times I faced magic of a darker kind. There were discipline issues, for example, and I sometimes found myself caring more than my students about the skills they would need to gain employment or go on to college. Perhaps most discouraging were the times when I would watch as more than a few students placed their essays into their notebooks, my comments unread, after glancing with mild interest at the grade at the top of their papers.

Conversely, as the sponsor of a club, whether the debate club, leadership club, or even as the sponsor of an activity such as the school newspaper, I found that my students' learning soared, as did my own. I was carried along with them on a wave of enthusiasm and energy, rather amazed at how hard students worked when the freedom and attendant responsibility became theirs alone. Many times I collapsed in a chair while waiting for the group to take "just a few more minutes" to finish a project—often a very challenging one, such as when they were editing a news piece for the school

**45**

paper or researching facts to make the perfect point in a staff editorial. They solicited comments from me about the content of their writing and asked for clarification about grammar issues. Because the tasks were theirs and they had assumed ownership of them, they cared enough to do them well.

This laser focus and devotion to learning is the result of a condition called engagement, and its power does not extend just to students. As we have seen in the first few chapters of this book, engagement is a component often lacking in professional development. When thinking about learning communities, perhaps we should consider them as clubs if we hope to gain the rich and autonomous learning that students enjoy when they become active members of such a group.

How important is engagement in literacy learning? Guthrie and Anderson's (1999) research found that students who are engaged develop deeper conceptual understandings and possess a greater sense of self-efficacy, the belief that one is capable of making a difference and the determination to do so. Self-efficacy increases motivation for learning and, in fact, drives results. *Engaging Adolescent Learners* (Lent 2006) provides a framework for helping students become motivated, independent learners as they gain the self-efficacy necessary for in-depth learning. Guthrie and Anderson use the term *self-determining* to define learners who have tapped into intrinsic motivation that leads to deeper and wider reading. They also cite the work of Glynn and Duit, who propose a model of conceptual learning based on extensive research.

## Glynn and Duit's Learning Conditions

♦ Existing knowledge is activated.

♦ New information and educational experiences are related to existing knowledge.

♦ Intrinsic motivation is developed.

♦ New knowledge is constructed.

♦ New knowledge is applied, evaluated, and revised. (Guthrie and Anderson 1999, 29)

The students involved in clubs were engaged in learning because Glynn and Duit's learning conditions were inherent in the authentic and meaningful tasks they tackled. I am reminded of a group of ninth graders who wanted to create a float for the school homecoming parade. They activated their existing knowledge by brainstorming all types of floats they were familiar with as a way of conceptualizing the term *float*. They began to apply new information to their prior knowledge by discussing the size and type of flatbed truck on which they would construct the float. Their motivation became solidly intrinsic as they planned the type of float they would construct, which, in turn, led to increased energy and resourcefulness. Each person left the first meeting tasked with gaining new information, such as how they could obtain a flatbed truck, whose parents would allow them to work on the float in their yard, and what type of materials they would need. They then used their new knowledge to create a float that exceeded their expectations and won them an award. Afterward, they evaluated the process by making notes in their scrapbook about what things they would do differently the following year when they built their tenth-grade float. These students probably would have denied that their float-building success was the result of their participation in a community of engaged "self-determined" learners, but that is exactly what they had become as they worked together toward their common goal.

As a faculty changes from a group of individuals who happen to be working in the same building to unified learning communities with a shared purpose, they must not only create effective learning conditions, but they must also understand two important components of successful groups: efficacy and engagement. Believing that they can make a difference will generate the necessary energy and engagement to do so. Robert Garmston, in a monthly column in the *Journal of Staff Development*, notes, "Groups with robust efficacy are likely to expend more energy, persevere longer, set more challenging goals, produce more learning, and continue in the face of failure" (2006, 73). Efficacy results when a group assumes control over its own decision making and believes that it can improve teaching practices and student learning. A faculty must become engaged in the process of learning in order to reap the benefits of efficacy, just as students must become engaged in the process of building a float to assume responsibility over its construction. While engagement often emerges unbidden as a group embarks on a challenging and meaningful task, it also can be created by understanding its characteristics. In fact, striving for engagement should be foundational in all teaching and learning practices.

## Characteristics of Engagement

To be surprised, to wonder, is to begin to understand.

—JOSE ORTEGA Y GASSET

### Engagement and Energy

When you become engaged in a task, whether weeding the garden or cooking a meal, energy supports that task and often is replenished by involvement in the activity itself. Such energy may be exclusive to the object of the engagement; for example, a person may have a sudden dip in energy when asked to perform a task in which he or she is disengaged, such as cleaning up the kitchen or studying for a test. Engagement is sustained by energy and, in fact, appears to produce it.

### Engagement and Social Contact

Guthrie and Anderson define reading engagement as "the joint functioning of motivation, conceptual knowledge, strategies, and social interactions" (1999, 20). This statement comes as no surprise to intuitive teachers. Enter any classroom in America and compare the engagement level of students sitting passively in desks and those same students in groups, actively learning. This principle is also in evidence when watching teachers working in isolation as opposed to those in collaboration.

### Engagement and Intrinsic Rewards

Deep engagement results from intrinsic rewards that offer solutions, information, or socially relevant interactions. Because human brains are constantly searching for meaning, the most compelling intrinsic reward is often satisfying curiosity or coming to understand something in a new way. Michael Fullan (2006) notes that intrinsic motivation involves passion, purpose, and energy, also important components of engagement itself. Intrinsic motivation is compounded when one is gaining knowledge that is relevant, meaningful, or altruistic.

### Engagement and Flow

When someone is deeply engaged in an activity that is neither too easy nor too difficult, he or she may enter into a state that Mihaly Csikszentmihalyi (1990), one of the world's leading researchers on positive psychology, defines as "flow." Time ceases to exist as the person narrows his or her attention and becomes totally absorbed in a task, especially one that stretches mental or physical abilities. It is the depth of concentration that creates this condition, and certain components are associated with it, such as the participant's perceiving the activity as meaningful and believing that he has some control over it. According to Csikszentmihalyi, a person who is in the flow experiences fulfillment and may gain such positive benefits as personal growth, skill development, and the ability to meet greater challenges. Smith and Wilhelm (2006), in their book *Going with the Flow,* examine Csikszentmihalyi's theories as they relate to engaging students in literacy learning.

These conditions of engagement cannot exist, of course, in an environment of fear. Energy is diffused by fear, social contact is stymied by fear, and flow stagnates in a state of fear. Fear often supports short-term extrinsic rewards but rarely drives long-term intrinsic motivation. Becoming aware of the conditions of engagement and removing any threats or fear is critical when establishing a learning community. Members of the community must feel safe if they are to engage in the process of examining deeply held beliefs, acknowledging their needs, and relating to each other in a way that will move the group toward authentic and sustained growth.

## Planning for Literacy Learning Communities

Perhaps the only true commonality that schools share is that they are each unique. Every student added to the student body, every teacher added to the faculty, every new administrator and staff member changes the complexion of the school. Every program, course, or extracurricular activity adds a shade that alters the school's impressionistic feel. The physical layout of the campus—its size, complexity, and physical attractiveness—adds a wash of color. Even the spiritual components of a school—its collective degree of empathy, deeply felt moral obligations, civic responsibility, or pride—contribute to its distinctiveness. Each literacy learning community, then, is born from its own schoolwide community and must enter this new world of professional development by recognizing and honoring the unique environment that produced it.

One of the reasons that long-term professional development initiatives are relatively easy to implement but extremely difficult to sustain is the ever-changing nature of schools. Initiatives that are bedrock today may be faint memories tomorrow, especially with leadership changes. In addition, sustainability is difficult because schools often do not allow adequate time for positive change to occur. Building relationships, forming trust, and engaging in reflective and deep dialogue will not happen in a twenty-minute faculty meeting or in the halls during class change. The commitment to content-area literacy learning must be viewed as one of the most important functions of a school, not simply as a professional development goal that will satisfy job requirements. Once a school commits itself to school-wide learning with communities that flow with the changing character of the school, a transformation will begin to occur with far-reaching, positive effects for everyone involved, from individual students to other schools in the system.

How long will it take for such a change to occur? Because of the individual nature of schools, there is no predictable time frame. Any professional development program that promises "results" in a set amount of time will lead to disappointment and counterproductive, hurried initiatives that may initially increase test scores but leave teachers and students frustrated and resentful. Such initiatives often create an environment that is constantly in a state of crisis rather than one of calm and reflective learning. As Thomas Guskey notes in *Evaluating Professional Development*, "The most worthwhile changes in education require time for adaptation, adjustment, and refinement" (2000, 9). Guskey points out that the first year is a time of experimentation, and "in the second year, efforts are typically more refined and efficient" (10). I have found that three years is a minimum for fostering the sustained learning necessary for positive change.

## Forming the Initial Literacy Learning Community

Leadership and learning are indispensable to each other.

—JOHN F. KENNEDY

Mandates rarely create engagement, nor are they of much value in forming learning communities. When faculty members are forced to add "one more thing" to their already overflowing plates, the spills aren't pretty—and principals often find that they have a huge mess to clean up. Prospective members should be assured from the very beginning that their contribution will be honored through release time or supplemental pay, and that their work will not be ignored or filed away in a folder labeled Literacy Learning Community. In fact, the group's contributions will form the backbone of the school's literacy initiatives. Although their participation will

# Three-Year Plan for Authentic, Embedded, and Sustained Literacy Learning Communities

## Year 1

*Authentic* literacy learning begins with the creation of a literacy team that acts as a learning community in its quest to understand fully the dynamics of literacy and the specialized needs of all students and staff. This is not a group charged with finding "best practices" for teachers as if they were seeking the most effective fertilizer to increase plant growth. Their task is not to become statisticians who will pore over facts and figures in an attempt to "narrow the gap" or raise test scores. This is a group whose focus is on learning, both their own and that of their students. Increased learning *will* lead to higher test scores, but if the primary goal is higher scores, the result may be shortsighted planning, superficial changes, and in some cases, unethical actions. Instead, this community will act as pioneers in a new type of professional development based on reflection, dialogue, and relationships as they seek knowledge and create a customized plan for meeting student learning needs.

## Year 2

*Embedded* literacy learning takes root as schoolwide learning communities develop, based on the original LLC, which will assist them in their growth. Such professional development scaffolding will incorporate Cambourne's Conditions of Learning: immersion, demonstration, expectation, responsibility, approximation, use, and response. As these embedded communities continue to develop, they will utilize a variety of staff development tools, such as study groups, coaching, and action research.

## Year 3

*Sustained* literacy learning will become the foundation of all school initiatives as the principles of learning are firmly established and employed by both students and faculty. This systemic process will be flexible enough to change as the school community adjusts, but constant enough to support ongoing, long-term growth and improvement. The goal is to enhance the very culture of the school through an engaging process that will leave the members revitalized and satisfied instead of drained and frustrated. See Figure 4.1 for an overview of Literacy Learning Communities.

require effort, members should expect something valuable in return—something intrinsically rewarding, an opportunity to form relationships with others in the school as they make personal contributions to students' increased learning. This committee will be afforded the respect due people whose expertise is valued. This is not a matter of sacrificing talents and time for the good of the school, as teachers are so often expected to do, but rather, it is an opportunity to engage in dialogue with like-minded professionals and make a genuine difference in the lives of students. It is a forum

# Overview of
# Literacy Learning Communities

| Literacy Learning Communities *Are* | Literacy Learning Communities *Are Not* |
|---|---|
| Focused on literacy learning | Obsessed with test scores |
| Open to all research about literacy | Restricted to the philosophy of one particular reading program |
| Guided by shared goals | Mandated by an administrator |
| Led by inquiry | Motivated by crisis |
| Strengthened through collaboration | Dissipated through competition |
| Committed to deep understanding | Satisfied with superficial knowledge |
| Informed by data | Driven by data |
| Secure in challenging the status quo | Fearful of "rocking the boat" |
| Comfortable with open deliberation | Restricted to the opinions of a few |

FIGURE 4.1

that nurtures, challenges, and provides a measure of control in a system that is often fraught with hopelessness and exacerbated by the sense that someone far away controls what happens in the classroom on a daily basis.

The first year of this three-year initiative is a time of exploration, but it is also a time to introduce the concept of literacy learning communities to the entire faculty. Although this embedded form of professional development is ongoing and may not include all members of the faculty for a few years, it is never too early to begin tapping into the advantages of professional learning communities by incorporating them at every opportunity.

Ideally, a knowledgeable principal should introduce literacy learning communities by devoting a faculty meeting or a scheduled inservice day to exploring the concept. What are professional learning communities? Literacy learning communities? In what ways do they differ from other committees? How does research support their role in increasing student learning? Faculty members should be told that their participation will require a year-long commitment and those who do not wish to engage in the initial literacy learning community will have opportunities in following years to participate. Most importantly, everyone should understand that

# Agenda to Introduce Literacy Learning Communities

1. Place faculty in groups to simulate an LLC. Provide chart paper and markers.
2. Ask groups to respond to one or more of the following and write their thoughts on chart paper:
   - What is learning?
   - What is achievement?
   - What is literacy?
   - What are the literacy strengths of our students?
   - What are the literacy needs of our students?
3. Allow each group to share their collective reflections.
4. Introduce the concept of LLCs . (Refer to Figure 4.1.)
5. Provide research from the first three chapters of this book showing how embedded professional learning in the form of LLCs will yield advantages for staff and students.
6. Discuss three-year plan:
   - Year 1—Initial literacy learning community will become a model for future learning communities.
   - Year 2—Embedded professional development will emerge as literacy learning communities increase schoolwide.
   - Year 3—Sustained learning communities will expand to students and others in the community.
7. Allow time for questions, concerns, and feedback

FIGURE 4.2

staff development in future years will be in the form of professional learning communities. See Figure 4.2 for a sample meeting agenda to introduce the concept of literacy learning communities.

After the meeting, each faculty member should receive an invitation similar to the one in Figure 4.3.

## Membership

Depending on the size of the school, the original literacy learning community should include no more than ten members. In small schools, as few as four or five people may make up the first LLC. In larger schools, two or

# Invitation to Join Initial Literacy Learning Community

Dear _____,

As you know, I am committed to student literacy learning, not simply for the purpose of raising test scores, but because I am aware of the importance of reading, writing, communicating, and learning across content areas. I am seeking a cross-section of the faculty, with representatives from various subjects and grades, if possible, to form the first literacy learning community. You do not need expertise in the area of literacy to join this group, but you must be willing to devote time to learning, collaborating, and engaging in study and dialogue. I hope to accommodate each person interested in becoming a member of this community and will expand the opportunity in future years so that everyone will eventually become a part of a literacy learning community (LLC).

The initial LLC will study and plan for deep student learning by assessing our students' literacy strengths and weaknesses, learning more about how to meet their needs, reevaluating existing practices, and sharing knowledge and insights with the rest of the faculty. Because this is a substantial commitment, you will be provided subs for meetings held during the school day and stipends for extended after-school meetings.

If you are interested in learning more about literacy and helping shape this school's future literacy goals, please respond in writing by (date). I appreciate your commitment to this important and exciting initiative.

Signed by principal

FIGURE 4.3

more communities may be needed to accommodate all who are interested. Membership may include, but not be limited to, the following:

**Initial LLC Membership**

Administrator (preferably the principal)

Reading coach

Content-area teachers

Special area or elective teachers

Media specialist

Guidance counselor or curriculum director

Paraprofessional

Student(s)

Parent, school board, or community member

It is more important to have members with a genuine interest in joining the learning community than to coerce someone from each of the categories to ensure wide representation. There is no one way of forming the "proper" membership. One high school team began its first year with a large percentage of reading teachers; another school did not have the media specialist as a part of the LLC for reasons unique to that school. Still another school ended up with a faculty member from each discipline, including art and band—and one of the elective teachers acted as chairperson.

The only nonnegotiable member of the team is an administrator, preferably the principal. One sure way to set the LLC up for failure is to have the group function without an administrator. In learning communities where the principal is absent, impotence often results. Members gain insights that never move beyond the epiphany stage, pertinent research gleaned from journals never translates into practice, and staff development plans remain as blueprints. Because this is a learn-before-taking-action initiative, the administrator must be a peer in the study process and contribute to the decisions of the group as colearner, not as manager.

In one middle school, the LLC examined their school's formal and informal data and determined that vocabulary was a significant weakness for their students. After studying the latest research regarding vocabulary acquisition, they formed a plan for staff development. The group thought it was important that faculty members understand how vocabulary affects comprehension and thus decided to provide the staff with a variety of ways to help students become independent and strategic in building their vocabulary skills. They targeted books from their professional library that addressed vocabulary and decided that Janet Allen's book *Words, Words, Words* would be the best resource to meet their needs. The principal, who had not taken an active role in the team, was concerned about the amount of time it was taking for the team to devise a plan. He felt that spending money on resources for students, rather than on professional books for staff, would be a better investment, despite the team's recommendation. He argued that a commercial vocabulary program for struggling readers or, at the very least, a set of dictionaries for each class would be a better use of the money, and expressed his view that students needed vocabulary instruction immediately to prepare them for upcoming standardized tests. As a result of the opposition, several members became discouraged and dropped out of the team. Eventually, the group stopped meeting, staff development returned to its previous "sit and get" state, and the principal resumed his role as the sole curriculum decision maker. Had this principal taken an active part in the team's learning, he would have understood why the group thought it necessary to provide teachers with resources outlining the role of vocabulary in literacy development before moving forward with student vocabulary programs. He would have read the research that shows that dictionaries alone are insufficient tools for vocabulary growth. He would have been a part of the dialogue that led this team to make their recommendations. Not only did this principal miss an opportunity to learn, he also effectively, although unintentionally, shut down members of the faculty who had become actively engaged in improving their school.

What about having students on the team? Many schools feel that faculty dialogue may be suppressed by the presence of students, but having students in the group, at least at some meetings, can provide much-needed insights for members as they study and plan literacy initiatives. One high school invited two students, one who was a voracious reader and the other who described himself as a "poor reader." These students became an invaluable part of the literacy community, offering new perspectives about their own learning as well as insights about effective instruction. They went on to form a very active student literacy team, which they dubbed a "club," with all the privileges and responsibilities of other clubs. They presented book talks on the morning news show, recommended titles for the media center, created thematic book displays, attended local reading conferences, created an unforgettable "Read Across America" book parade at a local elementary school, and sponsored a book fair to raise money for classroom libraries. The synergy between the student team and the adult team led to an unprecedented focus on literacy.

Once the members are gathered for the initial literacy learning committee meeting, they should elect a chair or cochairs to facilitate the meetings. A word of caution: Those who are in charge of everything else in the school generally are too busy to meet the demands of being the chairperson of this active group. Administrators, too, are usually poor choices as chairs because they should be seen as equal contributing members as the group develops into a democratic learning society. Next, the group should take as much time as necessary to establish guiding principles and bylaws that will support all actions the group takes. The following are suggested guiding principles and bylaws.

### Suggested LLC Guiding Principles

◆ Every member's voice will be heard and respected.

◆ Relationships and trust are paramount.

◆ Time will be provided for written or oral reflection during each meeting.

◆ Student learning will remain the focus of all study and action.

◆ Formal and informal data will inform decisions.

**Suggested LLC Bylaws**

◆ Duties of chair

◆ Positions within the team

◆ Calendar of meetings

◆ Decision-making processes

◆ Norms for disagreement

◆ Process for sharing work

Members should meet at least once a week for an hour and once a month for an extended period, preferably a half or whole day. This time is essential not only to build and maintain relationships but also for the time-consuming work of collecting data to guide members' learning and helping them decide on appropriate actions to increase student learning.

As much as possible, it is also important to include social activities in the planning of meetings. Refreshments, music, and time for conversation, at either the beginning or end of the meeting, are vital in providing a positive and productive atmosphere as members engage in collaborative work. There also should be opportunities for stories about classroom interactions and time for sharing student work, as well as readings from favorite books, articles, or poetry.

The environment of a literacy team is one of its most important attributes. Because learning, by definition, is a process that ebbs and flows with the acquisition of new knowledge, learning communities must also be fluid, almost experimental. Their goal is one of inquiry and discovery, as members constantly gain and adapt information. They may not know what will work at first, and they may find that what works with one group of students may not work with another. It is the dialogue, reflection, and freedom to risk in both individual thinking and collective actions that will allow this community to grow in ways that will transcend the status quo. If it is to develop a sense of shared purpose, collegiality, and common understanding, the team must cultivate a space for such a process to occur. Members should be encouraged to throw off the stiff robes of mandates and directives and return to learning as a creative and nurturing process.

# Picture of a Literacy Learning Community

**Participation**
- ◆ Should be voluntary
- ◆ Should be within a social as well as an academic setting
- ◆ Should be energy producing, not energy draining

**Members**
- ◆ Should be provided with release time or supplemental pay
- ◆ Should be rewarded with learning opportunities, such as attending conferences or visits to other schools and districts
- ◆ Should be the literacy decision-making branch of the school

**Tasks**
- ◆ Should be decided by the team
- ◆ Should be directly tied to student learning
- ◆ Should be evenly divided based on member strengths

**Literacy**
- ◆ Should be infused into each meeting
- ◆ Should be within the context of a joyful, lifelong pursuit
- ◆ Should be targeted across the curriculum

Once that happens, they will recognize the value of being a part of an endeavor that forges relationships, tills common ground, and celebrates literacy.

## Questions for Reflection

1. What factors may discourage you from becoming a part of a literacy learning community?

2. How could participation in a learning community make your school life easier?

3. How do you view the role of literacy in content-area classes?

4. What one area of literacy do you want to know more about?

5. Where do you see this school three years from now? Where do you see yourself?

## Reflection Through Action

Experience the concept of literacy learning communities by forming groups for the purpose of reading a common book, engaging in dialogue about it, and taking some action after the group finishes the book. For this exercise, faculty members may choose their own groups and their own reading selections, taking several weeks to finish the book. Then, in place of regularly held faculty meetings or department meetings, or during scheduled inservice days, groups will discuss their reading and decide on the action they will take related to the reading.

### Suggested Books and Activities for Experimental Literacy Learning Communities

1. Book: *The Curious Incident of a Dog in the Night-Time*, by Mark Haddon. This best-selling novel is written from the viewpoint of an autistic adolescent.

   Action: Create a flyer on autism to distribute to the staff.

2. Book: *The Demon in the Freezer*, by Richard Preston. This nonfiction book about the history and physical effects of anthrax and smallpox is especially interesting to science teachers.

   Action: Organize a student study group using the same book. Science teachers will explain the biological processes referred to in the book— or have students read and discuss a young adult novel that addresses the same topic: *Code Orange*, by Caroline Cooney.

3. Book: *Feed* by M. T. Anderson. A National Book Award Finalist. This book is about a future world where teens' abilities to read, write, and think have been diminished by transmitters implanted in their brains.

   Action: Decide how the novel could be used in classroom instruction.

4. Book: *Freakonomics: A Rogue Economist Explores the Hidden Side of Everything*, by Steven Levitt and Stephen Dubner. This nonfiction book exemplifies the art of inquiry by taking a second look at data and asking questions that require thinking in different ways.

Action: Pull out amazing facts and conundrums and present to students as exercises in critical thinking.

5. Book: *Maus: A Survivor's Tale*, Art Spiegelman's graphic novel. This book introduces readers to a Jewish survivor of the Holocaust. The book was the winner of the 1992 Pulitzer Prize.

   Action: Provide the faculty with ways in which graphic novels could be used to support content-area study.

## Study Group Resources: Creating a Learning Community

- *Teaching as the Learning Profession: Handbook of Policy and Practice* (Darling-Hammond and Sykes 1999)

- *Leadership Capacity for Lasting School Improvement* (Lambert 2003)

- *Connecting Leadership with Learning* (Copeland and Knapp 2006)

- *Getting Started: Reculturing Schools to Become Professional Learning Communities* (Eaker, DuFour, and DuFour 2002)

- *Learning Together, Leading Together: Changing Schools Through Professional Learning Communities* (Hord 2003)

# Assessing Literacy Learning Needs

The teacher is no longer merely the one who teaches,
but one who is himself taught in dialogue with the
students, who in turn while being taught also teaches.

—PAULO FREIRE

It was the first meeting of this large middle school's literacy learning community. Teachers representing each department, including a math teacher who admitted that reading was not "her thing," sat in the conference room around two large tables that had been pulled together, warm sunlight reflecting off whiteboards that lined the walls. We heard the bell ring that signaled the beginning of the school day and waited for the morning announcements to end. Instead of calling roll, answering multiple questions simultaneously, smiling at the same joke they had heard five times the day before, telling one more student to please remember to sharpen his pencil before class begins, taking up forms for the front office, and quickly scanning the day's lesson plans, these teachers were sitting quietly, talking among themselves about the daily events that make up their classroom lives. Soon they began laughing about incidents involving students, their stories rivaling those of television sitcoms, and then, as if they were a single entity, they became sad and serious as they discussed how a student was coping with the death of his parent. I felt privileged to be a temporary member of this group, almost a voyeur, witnessing the deeply entrenched relationships, and I looked forward to the coming year when their bonds would strengthen and their powerful energy would be harnessed into motion.

Each day teachers enter a world as fast-paced as that of the busiest Wall Street stockbroker, so it is especially difficult for them to engage in the slow and sometimes tedious process of assessing their literacy needs. In addition, as teachers tell me constantly, "I have this entire curriculum to cover (arms spread wide to indicate just how much there is to be covered) and you're asking me to slow down? I need to speed up!" Principals who use professional development dollars to provide substitutes so teachers can have uninterrupted time together must believe that an all-day meeting will result in increasing student learning. They also must be patient, however, and value the long-term, sustained benefits of this type of community-building process rather than the short-lived, initial flare-ups of traditional professional development.

Although members of the middle school's literacy learning community understood the importance of deliberative planning, they instinctively wanted to jump to solutions. As a creative and energetic group accustomed to taking action, it was difficult for them to engage in reflection, a necessary precursor to action. I felt them straining to move forward. They knew what was going on in their classrooms, they knew their students, and they knew they could "fix" the problem if they only had time, something that was being provided to them on this day. Such a culture is prevalent in most secondary schools because *it is the way things have always been.* As a consultant, my biggest challenge would be to help the group move into a more reflective cycle, one that would lead them toward inquiry about the most important challenges to their students' literacy learning.

As we began our first meeting, I provided each member of the learning community with a tangible place for their learning to be housed. A tabbed binder, one with rings that spring loudly open, became a portfolio where members could keep notes, handouts, and student work samples. I asked the group to think about a symbol of learning that would remind them of their purpose in meeting with this community, one they might want to place under the clear, plastic cover on the front of the notebook. An art teacher offered suggestions of graphics that would tie the school mascot to student learning. Others joined in, creating puns and acronyms that ranged from the obscene to the painfully obvious. The group began laughing, building their community's foundation with strong planks of collegial relationships. I wrote the words *Literacy Learning* on one of the whiteboards and asked individuals to freewrite in their notebooks. "What does this term mean to you?" I picked up a pen and begin to write as well, delving anew into topics I have examined countless times, and found, as always, that writing brings me to greater understanding.

# Dialogue

*To the Greeks dia-logos meant a free-flowing of meaning through
a group, allowing the group to discover insights not attainable
individually.*

— PETER SENGE, *THE FIFTH DISCIPLINE*

My goal was to jump-start the cycle of reflection through writing and then
ask members of the group to engage in dialogue as a catalyst for deeper
thinking. Such discourse often requires extended conversations as members learn to suspend judgments and long-held beliefs in order to fairly
consider another's perspective. This is not to say, of course, that you
should waffle on issues that are a deeply held part of your value system or
change positions simply to be agreeable. Rather, this is about members
embracing paradox and ambiguity in an effort to stretch thinking or, as
Ellinor and Gerard (1998), in their book *Dialogue: Rediscover the Transforming Power of Conversation*, term it, having a "shift of mind" that will
move them away from either/or thinking and open the doors to collective
problem solving. Peter Senge uses a word in his work, "metanoia," which
means a "fundamental shift or change, or more literally transcendence of
mind." He points out that the purpose of dialogue is to "go beyond any one
individual's understanding" and to "explore complex difficult issues from
many points of view" (1990, 241). Dialogue has the power to profoundly
change the way people talk to each other and the way they consider important issues. It has the power to re-create thinking and learning.

Dialogue doesn't simply happen because a group of people engages in a
conversation. It is a type of talk that can move people intellectually, emo-
tionally, and often spiritually as they are exposed to the ideas of those with
whom they are interacting. Groups should spend time thinking about the
nature of dialogue, as its principles will be foundational in this group's
communication. The list on page 64 highlights the habits that can be cultivated to establish an atmosphere of respect and a culture of thoughtful
inquiry and effective dialogue.

I ask group members to underline the most important idea in their
freewriting about literacy learning and share with the rest of the group by
reading it aloud or paraphrasing so that others may respond to their
thoughts. Many of the same concepts addressed in Chapter 3 may appear
as part of the discussion. This initial communication marks the beginning
of a dialogue that will become a systemic part of the group's identity. As

## Habits of Effective Dialogue

◆ Judgment is suspended.
◆ Listening is paired with empathy and understanding.
◆ Examination of issues trumps defense of viewpoints.
◆ Inquiry guides questions and comments.
◆ Silence is accepted.
◆ Assumptions are re-examined.
◆ Spontaneity is encouraged.
◆ Control is diminished.
◆ Perspectives are broadened.
◆ Ambiguity is expected.
◆ Differences are respected.
◆ Respect is bedrock.

they listen thoughtfully to each other and consider perspectives they may not have thought about before, they are creating a shared commitment to know more about literacy, one that will soon grow into a common purpose

As facilitator, I try unobtrusively to guide the group toward productive dialogue if they begin to stream into areas outside their *circle of influence*, Stephen Covey's (1989) term for those things over which we have no real control. In one high school, for example, members of the literacy team could not seem to move past the issue of society's influence on the learning habits of their students. While such a topic was certainly worth noting, especially if members found it to be significant, it became clear that there was nothing the group could do about this particular problem. It was important for them to shift from their circle of concern back into their circle of influence, the areas over which they had control, if they were going to take actions that would directly affect the learning of their students.

Figure 5.1 offers questions that will guide the conversation and help keep the group focused as they begin to assess their school's literacy culture. The group's recorder should take notes on chart paper as members use the questions as prompts in considering all aspects of literacy learning. It also is helpful if someone records notes on a computer at the same time and sends the document to members later. If there is not a clear answer to one of the questions, mark it as one that may need further investigation.

# Assessing Literacy Culture

1. How is literacy defined by students in this school? How is it defined by teachers?

2. What are students' attitudes toward literacy in general, reading and writing in particular?

3. What are the teachers' attitudes toward literacy?

4. What does it mean to learn?

5. To what extent are Cambourne's Conditions of Learning (see pages 38–39) in place in most classrooms?

6. To what extent is differentiated instruction a part of our school learning culture?

   ◆ How are the needs of struggling readers being met?

   ◆ How are the needs of advanced readers being met?

   ◆ How are the needs of students with various learning styles being met?

7. To what extent is the schoolwide community (parents, alumni/ae, business, or education partners) involved in students' literacy learning?

8. What are students' attitudes toward standardized testing?

9. What are teachers' attitudes toward standardized testing?

10. What are administrators' attitudes toward standardized testing?

11. How much time is devoted to test prep activities in content-area classrooms?

12. How are the results of standardized tests used?

13. What types of assessments are used in content-area classes?

   ◆ Tests from textbook publishers

   ◆ Teacher-made tests

   ◆ Portfolios

   ◆ Alternative assessments (i.e., oral, project-based, collaborative presentations)

   ◆ Essays or written papers

   ◆ Self-assessment

14. How does assessment inform instruction in content-area classes?

15. What literacy resources/opportunities are available to students?

   ◆ Classroom libraries containing a wide and diverse selection of fiction and nonfiction

   ◆ Primary documents

   ◆ Visual text

   ◆ Technology

   ◆ Classes or extracurricular activities in journalism, speech, art, TV production, advanced technology, business, drama, reading, or creative writing

*(Continues)*

FIGURE 5.1

◆ Well-stocked and accessible media center

◆ Speakers, videos, or extracurricular experiences related to content-area studies

◆ Authentic and relevant projects requiring research

16. What supplemental literacy resources are available to content-area teachers?

◆ Current events periodicals

◆ Videos

◆ Technology

◆ Professional library (containing professional books and journals)

◆ Supplemental texts

17. To what extent do content-area teachers address the following components of literacy?

◆ Students' background knowledge

◆ Word study (using context clues, analyzing word parts, assessing familiarity)

◆ Comprehension skills (summarizing, clarifying, predicting, monitoring comprehension)

◆ Text structure (fiction and nonfiction)

◆ The writing process (prewriting, revising, editing)

◆ Student choice in reading and/or writing topics

◆ Critical thinking

◆ Communication skills

18. To what extent do content-area teachers incorporate the following instructional practices?

◆ Collaborative learning

◆ Differentiated learning

◆ Project-based learning

◆ Activities/projects that require deep and critical thinking

◆ Discussions

◆ Writing to learn

◆ Scaffolding instruction

◆ Modeling effective reading practices (read-alouds or think-alouds)

19. What packaged reading programs does the school use? To what extent are they effective?

20. To what extent is interdisciplinary or cross-curricular learning a part of content-area study?

21. Does the school incorporate sustained silent reading or time for independent reading?

22. To what extent are learners motivated or engaged in reading, writing, or learning?

23. To what extent is literacy used for social causes or civic purposes?

FIGURE 5.1 *continued*

The dialogue that emerges from these prompts is crucial to the eventual study of the literacy learning community. Members should not be rushed as they examine each item; instead, they should be encouraged to provide examples that support their observations or beliefs. Groups sometimes become bogged down because they will determine that some areas of the school engage in a practice; for example, independent reading in English classes, but that same practice may be nonexistent in other areas of the school. They often don't know how to assess a practice if it isn't common throughout the school. In such cases, the group should simply note where it most frequently occurs and where it is absent. Detailed notes or questions under each category will help if members decide to return to a specific topic at a later time. The goal during this phase of the process is for the group to develop, as much as possible, a three-dimensional image of literacy as it exists in the school, although the picture may come in and out of focus depending upon what part of the school's population is being examined. Each bit of information will, however, fill in the blanks and help the group understand the literacy practices, habits, and attitudes of everyone within the school community.

## Collecting Data

> Our knowledge of the world comes from gathering around great things in a complex and interactive community of truth.
>
> —PARKER PALMER, *THE COURAGE TO TEACH*

The next step is to reexamine the particulars of the dialogue, as the group reviews all notes together. Members should now return to any important item about which they had too little information to assess. For example, it may be difficult to know students' attitudes about literacy or teachers' instructional practices. An effective way to collect this information is through a survey, such as the one in Figure 3.1. Other questions may be added to that survey in an effort to gain specific information regarding attitudes toward literacy. Here are sample survey questions regarding students' attitudes toward literacy.

◆ How important is the ability to read well?

◆ To what extent, if any, do good readers have an advantage over those who struggle with reading?

◆ How important are reading skills in passing content-area classes?

- How have your reading habits changed from elementary school to middle school? Middle school to high school?

- Why do you read?

- If you don't spend much time reading, why not?

- In what ways do you use the media center? How often do you use it?

A survey like this one would be useful in assessing teachers' instructional practices as well, *if* teachers trusted that the information they provide would not be used in punitive ways. In order to gain a complete picture of the school's literacy needs, the group also should examine standardized test scores, reading and writing scores on diagnostic tests, attendance records, and any other pertinent information.

A word about data: Data should exist to serve us, not to become our master. Data without a human connection is as useless as sperm in a test tube. It has the potential to reveal important information regarding the learning needs and strengths of students and of the school collectively, but without being enveloped within the context of the whole person, it can be a savage deceiver. There is no doubt that data can be used to construct new and relevant learning when it shows valid areas of need or gaps in knowledge, but it can also be used to destroy the fragile hold that some students have on their existing knowledge, self-esteem, or view of themselves as learners.

I have been in schools where the reading coach is used as a data repository, spending most of her time in an office lined with bookshelves filled with unused young adult novels. Such coaches spend their time manipulating and remanipulating the reams of data that cross their desks daily. Education has become so data driven that we sometimes forget that human beings are more than data suppliers. Even quantitative data relies on a human element that can skew the results or make it completely invalid. Students are famous for "Christmas treeing" standardized tests or doing well at the beginning of a test only to drift off toward the end, providing results that are simply worthless. In addition, data may merely reflect a student's bad day, lack of background knowledge about a topic, or a problem with test anxiety. It is, therefore, important to look at all types of data to gain a comprehensive portrait of the literacy culture of the school and its students' literacy needs. Schools should monitor themselves to make sure they are being data informed, not data driven. The following list contains types of data that may be helpful in assessing the school's literacy culture.

## Data to Determine Student Literacy Needs

- ◆ Judgment is suspended.
- ◆ Interviews
- ◆ Surveys
- ◆ Teacher observation notes
- ◆ Student work samples
- ◆ Whole-class evaluations
- ◆ Student responses to programs or assignments
- ◆ Portfolios
- ◆ Library check-out records
- ◆ Attendance records
- ◆ Informal Reading Inventories
- ◆ Teacher-made tests
- ◆ Standardized test scores
- ◆ Diagnostic test scores
- ◆ Professional development records
- ◆ Inventories of literacy resources
- ◆ Individual case studies

## *Organizing and Evaluating Data*

The only real evaluation is whether students learn more.

—BRUCE JOYCE AND BEVERLY SHOWERS, *STUDENT
ACHIEVEMENT THROUGH STAFF DEVELOPMENT*

Once the group is satisfied that they have reviewed all significant aspects of the school's literacy culture, they should begin organizing their notes and data into categories and/or subcategories. Column 1 in Figure 5.2 gives examples of possible categories. Plastic bins, notebooks, folders, or boxes can provide a system for separating information physically into easily accessible categories. Once the data is organized and examined, the group will be in a position to decide which aspect of literacy would be most beneficial for their study. Members should remind themselves that the focus of their work is always on increasing student learning.

| Literacy Component | Positive aspect of the school | Satisfactory aspect of the school | Not applicable | Weak aspect of the school | Absent or severely deficient |
|---|---|---|---|---|---|
| Attitude | | | | | |
| Motivation Engagement | | | | | |
| Learning Conditions | | | | | |
| Differentiated Instruction | | | | | |
| Assessment | | | | | |
| Parental Involvement | | | | | |
| Community Involvement | | | | | |
| *Literacy Resources for Students | | | | | |
| *Literacy Resources for Teachers | | | | | |
| *Technology | | | | | |
| *Reading Strategies | | | | | |
| *Instructional Practices | | | | | |

*Individual components of category may be listed separately

FIGURE 5.2 *Evaluating Components of Literacy*

© 2007 by ReLeah Cossett Lent from *Literacy Learning Communities*. Portsmouth, NH: Heinemann.

There are several ways for the group to determine which area of study should be targeted, or whether the large group should break into smaller learning communities to address different topics. A chart such as the one shown in the table in Figure 5.2 may help members initially narrow the choices for study. Other ways to choose the focus of study is to provide each member with three colored sticky dots. Members place the three dots on three different topics they believe warrant study, or they may place all their dots on one area if they feel strongly that that one topic is most important. The areas with the most dots reflect the consensus of the group.

While this process may appear to be burdensome, it actually falls into place rather quickly if members have spent sufficient time assessing each area individually. In one school, the assessment of virtually every component of literacy led the team back to the same issue: student motivation. This school was in a high socioeconomic area and many of their students had received enrichment at home, as well as in their elementary and middle schools. Formal data analysis revealed that very few students had significant problems with reading comprehension or vocabulary, and yet teachers were reporting that students seemed interested only in grades, not in learning. As members delved into informal data, they confirmed that students could read, but wouldn't; could write, but wanted to "get by" with only the minimum required. Teacher and student surveys revealed that students were unmotivated and unengaged in most content-area studies. Their real interests lay in after-school work or social activities. Once the team understood the challenge, they became immersed in research on motivation and engagement in an effort to take appropriate action to help students tap into their full learning potential. If the group had not taken the time to examine all aspects of their school's literacy culture, they may have targeted a study focus such as reading comprehension, which was not actually a significant need.

It is important that the group understand that the topic they choose will not make or break this initiative. The process of assessing their school's literacy learning needs will increase their collegiality and knowledge of and commitment to literacy, as will the extended dialogue that accompanies the study. In addition, the data they collect will be available for use by various segments of the school population in staff development or school improvement plans. In future years, as literacy learning communities expand throughout the school, the work done by this initial literacy learning community will be invaluable in helping them address other areas of study. Figure 5.3 reviews the process for determining the area of study.

## Process for Determining Area of Study

| Steps in Process | Description |
| --- | --- |
| Engage in Dialogue | The group will assess the literacy attitudes, resources, and practices of every segment of the school community by engaging in a dialogue about the various components of each. Use Figure 5.2 as an assessment guide. |
| Collect Data | The group will collect data, both formal and informal, that "fills in the blanks" and creates a comprehensive picture of the school's literacy needs and strengths. See Figure 5.2 for examples of data. |
| Categorize and Assess Data | The group will develop a system for categorizing data and assessing it to determine the literacy area of need that will become the focus of study. See Figure 5.2 for an example of how to evaluate components of literacy. |

FIGURE 5.3

Literacy learning communities will develop and strengthen as members work together to seek the truth about their students, staff, and school. They must objectively and thoroughly examine what exists to understand what is possible. The process of learning begins with the first meeting as members recognize that each piece of information, each observation, each shift in thinking, and each comment made by their colleagues will help them discover how they can best prepare their students to embark on their own journeys toward becoming joyfully literate adults.

## Questions for Reflection

1. What is your initial reaction to the word *data?*

2. How does data inform your instruction on a daily basis?

3. How do you feel about how standardized testing data is used to determine students' academic progress?

4. What dialogue have you had with a colleague that has affected your life as a teacher or administrator?

5. What do you see as the most important aspect of literacy in the lives of students today?

## *Reflection Through Action*

For groups that are ready to go beyond the basics in literacy, see www.21stcenturyskills.org for a framework of twenty-first-century learning. Assess your school's literacy in the following areas:

- Twenty-first-century literacy content
    - Global awareness
    - Financial, economic, business, and entrepreneurial literacy
    - Civic literacy
    - Health and awareness
- Students' learning and thinking skills in content-area classes
    - Critical thinking and problem-solving skills
    - Communication skills
    - Creativity and innovation skills
    - Collaboration skills
    - Contextual learning skills
    - Information and media literacy skills
- The school's information and communications technology (ICT) literacy
    - Ability of our students to use technology to learn content and skills
    - Ability of students to know *how* to learn, think critically, solve problems, use information, communicate, innovate, and collaborate
- How life skills are being addressed in all subject areas
    - Leadership
    - Ethics
    - Accountability
    - Adaptability

◆ Personal productivity

◆ Personal responsibility

◆ People skills

◆ Self-direction

◆ Social responsibility

## Study Group Resources: Assessing Literacy Learning

◆ *Beyond the Numbers: Making Data Work for Teachers and School Leaders* (White 2005)

◆ *Collaborative Analysis of Student Work: Improving Teaching and Learning* (Langer, Colton, and Goff 2003)

◆ *The Handbook of Literacy Assessment and Evaluation*, 2nd ed. (Harp 2000)

◆ *Student Involved Classroom Assessment*, 3rd ed. (Stiggins 2001)

◆ *Using Data to Assess Your Reading Program* (Calhoun 2004)

# 6

# *Developing a Literacy Learning Plan*

We're embarking on a long journey that never ends. I
am sixty-nine years old as I write these words and I know
I will continue on this search until the end of life itself.
Indeed, it is the journey that counts, not the destination.

—DONALD GRAVES, *THE ENERGY TO TEACH*

Walton Middle School is a sprawling campus within walking distance of a large, picturesque lake that serves as a town square for the small community of DeFuniak Springs, Florida. While this school would not be categorized as an inner-city school, its racial and socioeconomic blend gives it a flavor that distinguishes it from the other, more rural schools that populate the district. The school is fortunate to have a knowledgeable onsite reading coach and a principal who is open to new ideas. As a literacy consultant, one of my first tasks was to help the school's initial literacy learning community, called the Reading Leadership Team, create a literacy plan. The group, composed of the principal; the district reading coach; the onsite reading coach; two reading teachers; the media specialist; and one teacher each from science, social studies, math, language arts, and PE, was energetic, funny, and willing to take academic risks. The principal, Russell Hughes, was affectionate toward his teachers and assumed the role of colearner in this process. The group was anxious to get down to work, so after establishing ground rules and guiding principles, we began going through the process of assessing the school's literacy needs and strengths, filling up several whiteboards as the group's brainstorming led them simultaneously in many different directions.

It was hard to keep this vivacious group focused because each member had multiple ideas, and I had little doubt that, given enough time, they could have handled the school's problems single-handedly. I punctuated the dialogue by reading aloud to them from young adult novels to provide a mental break from the rather intense brainstorming. For example, we laughed aloud at a passage from Gordon Korman's *No More Dead Dogs*, where a teacher insists that one of his favorite books (a "timeless classic" where the dog dies) should also be his students' favorite book. For the most part, the members shared a genuine love of books and they eagerly wrote down titles of books they wanted to use with their students.

As the day progressed, the team returned repeatedly to what has sometimes been described as an "itch," or a "pebble in the shoe," a bothersome issue that demands attention. A careful listener will recognize when this phenomenon occurs because members will allude to the topic repeatedly, even though at first it may not carry a consistent strand in the dialogue. Then someone will eventually address the topic directly, delving a bit deeper into it; finally, it will permeate every aspect of the conversation. That is the signal to stop absentmindedly scratching and take a look at the source of the itch. In this case, the itch was parental involvement. As the group examined their data, they saw that both the district reading coach and the onsite reading coach had worked with content-area teachers on strategies that would improve students' reading abilities. The principal had initiated a sustained silent reading time schoolwide and provided resources and materials that helped both students and the faculty better understand the process of reading. The knowledge was in place, but teachers felt the missing piece was the lack of support from home. In many cases, students were not receiving adequate help outside of school to reinforce either the love of reading or the frequent practice it would take to improve their reading skills. I suggested that the group survey the students *and* parents to determine if their observations were correct.

During the next several weeks, the faculty surveyed the entire student body in an effort to determine how literacy was incorporated into the home environment. Students were asked how often they read at home, what types of magazines were available to them, and whether their parents received the newspaper, as well as questions about their overall reading habits outside of school. The parents were also surveyed, and although the response was not overwhelming, the group had enough information to determine that reading support at home was spotty at best.

Armed with the results of the surveys, the group decided to find out more about family literacy. They read articles about its importance in a successful schoolwide literacy program and contacted the Florida Coalition of Literacy, a statewide group that helps schools incorporate family and community literacy. The next phase was to determine how they could educate parents about the importance of reading with their children.

After another session of brainstorming, the group finally came up with an idea they dubbed Dancing Through Literacy. They knew what a powerful motivator dancing was for their students, so they decided to tie this positive activity to their goal of increasing parental involvement. They decided that the event, which was to be held during the evening, would be a family affair; the only way students would be admitted was if at least one parent or guardian accompanied them.

The group divided the tasks, invited other faculty members to participate, publicized the event, and the pieces fell into place. On the cool January night when parents arrived in the school's parking lot, they were greeted by huge lights that led the way to the cafeteria, where they registered. Guests received a colored key that would designate how they would travel from session to session later in the evening. Their child was escorted to the gym to dance the evening away with a DJ. There were door prizes and refreshments—and, of course, books.

The faculty was thrilled to count over seventy parents walking through the cafeteria doors, a far cry from the usual five or ten who appeared on regular parent/teacher nights. The evening began with a welcome from Mr. Hughes and the drawing of door prizes for parents. Pat Nease, a professional storyteller, entertained the group with a hilarious personification of two married socks who, sadly, became separated in the washing machine. After refreshments, more drawings, and a visit to the book fair where the district reading coach and media specialist helped parents choose books for their children, it was time to get down to business. The colored keys that parents had been given earlier determined which session parents would attend first.

One of the sessions was led by Cynthia Goodsen, an Exceptional Student Education (ESE) teacher who provided a PowerPoint presentation on the importance of parents reading with their children. The research was presented in a compelling and understandable way that left no doubt that the practice of reading is, obviously, one of the best ways to create lifelong, proficient readers. The second session was led by a local high school teacher, Billy Moore, also a popular author. He discussed his writing and the background of his books, specifically his most popular book for adolescents, *Cracker's Mule.* The onsite reading coach, Dr. Dale Yount, led the third session, showing parents how to help their children with critical thinking by analyzing cartoons.

By all accounts, the night was a huge success, one that parents wanted to see repeated. In fact, when parents were asked for written feedback about the night, the only negative comment was that the evening was not long enough.

When I returned to the school for our final meeting of the year, the group was in high gear—still ebullient as they described the success of Dancing Through Literacy. Their collaboration and shared purpose over the past several months led to a synergy that was tangible and contagious. They immediately began organizing their notes and the parents' feedback so it would be accessible for next year's event. Each of the group members had a story to tell—about how much their students loved the event to comments from parents that affirmed the importance of the project. Cynthia Goodsen, the teacher who had led one of the sessions that evening, shared an unexpected exchange with a parent.

> [A] father approached me after my presentation. He asked me what help there was for an adult who could not read. He explained his job required technical expertise and he had learned to read just enough to get by. As tears welled up in his eyes, he said that he wanted to be able to help his daughter with her homework but was unable to read her seventh-grade textbooks. Trying unsuccessfully to restrain my own emotions, I showed him some reading websites and wrote down local contact information for adult literacy programs. I thanked him for his courage in seeking out help—and the opportunity he had given me to guide him in the right direction.

This story led to expanded dialogue about ways the school could offer literacy services to parents who might need them. The team is now in the process of documenting how the evening's activities may have increased literacy support at home and to what extent such support has helped their students become better readers.

At the end of the meeting as I was packing up my materials, I watched some of the members of Walton Middle School's Reading Leadership Team, the epitome of a literacy learning community, put on their walking shoes and step out into the brilliant spring afternoon. They were headed toward the lake, intending to get in a mile or so of walking exercise before going home. As I listened to their laughter floating back to me across the campus, I was infused with hope.

## Developing a Literacy Learning Plan

> A little knowledge that acts is worth infinitely more than much knowledge that is idle.
>
> — Kahlil Gibran, Lebanese poet

As I recall the experience of Walton Middle School, I am reminded of Glynn and Duit's Learning Conditions (see Chapter 4).

◆ Existing knowledge is activated.

◆ New information and educational experiences are related to existing knowledge.

◆ Intrinsic motivation is developed.

◆ New knowledge is constructed.

◆ New knowledge is applied, evaluated, and revised.

Walton Middle School followed the model as if it were their blueprint, although they had no directions other than their own intuitive sense of learning. It has become clear to me that authentic learning will inherently follow such a plan — for adults and for students. Whenever I find successful examples of learning resulting in actions that make a difference in the lives of students, adults or other communities, I can trace both Cambourne's Conditions of Learning (Chapter 3, page 40) and Glynn and Duit's Learning Conditions through the process. I also am reminded of the importance of developing a shared purpose, as this element often catapults the community into taking action far beyond anything a single individual could accomplish alone, no matter how smart, talented, or creative he or she happens to be.

How, then, can literacy learning communities develop that common goal and engage in authentic learning that leads to significant change for the entire school? The group must remain focused on collective learning directly related to students' needs rather than shortcutting the process in favor of collecting initial "gains," such as increased test scores. They must continuously remind each other that learning itself is the potion that will work the magic.

Remaining focused requires discipline, commitment, and a definitive plan of action. The following questions will help the group develop and execute action based upon their ongoing learning.

## Questions for a Plan of Action

◆ What is the focus of the study?

◆ What factors/data led the group to determine the focus?

◆ How, specifically, will the group's study improve student learning?

◆ How will the study translate into or dovetail with some type of action?

◆ What does the group hope to learn from its study/action?

◆ What resources or materials will the group need in order to embark upon its study?

◆ How will the group know that their action has been effective in improving student learning?

The very nature of learning communities requires that each group engage in enough introspection to gain a fairly good idea of who they are and the road they should travel. Because the content of each learning action plan will look entirely different based on the unique elements of the school, what follows are merely examples of Learning Action Plans that a literacy learning community, especially the initial LLC, might undertake to increase student learning and, at the same time, act as models for LLCs that will emerge schoolwide in following years. I provide these examples as springboards, since groups must rely on their own practices of inquiry and dialogue to tap into their diverse talents, collective intelligence, and creativity as they form plans of action that will permeate their school's distinctive literacy culture. Figure 6.1 presents a template for a Learning Action Plan.

## Example 1: Learning Action Plan to Address Urgent Literacy Need

As LLCs assess their literacy needs, they may discover that they need to take immediate actions either to address an urgent issue or to facilitate

# Learning Action Plan

Focus of Study _____

Goal of Learning _____

Goal of Action _____

Resources _____

Method of Study _____

Actions Resulting from Learning

Time Frame for Action _____

Dissemination of Learning

Assessment of Action

FIGURE 6.1

© 2007 by ReLeah Cossett Lent from *Literacy Learning Communities*. Portsmouth, NH: Heinemann.

maximum student learning. For example, if data indicates that many of their students are deficient in vocabulary skills, the group may decide to delve into the topic of vocabulary, study current research, and create an action plan for increasing students' vocabulary skills as soon as possible. A plan of study and action may look similar to the following.

## Focus of Study

◆   Vocabulary

## Goal of Learning

◆   The LLC will learn how effective vocabulary instructional practices can help students become independent word learners.

## Goal of Action

◆   The LLC will learn to utilize a variety of instructional practices that will aid students in improving vocabulary skills.

## Resources

◆   Onsite reading coach, district reading specialist, consultant

◆   Professional journal articles related to vocabulary research

   ◆   "Assessing and Supporting Independent Word Learning Strategies of Middle School Students" (Harmon 2000)

   ◆   "Assisting Struggling Readers in Building Vocabulary and Background Knowledge" (Irvin 2001)

   ◆   "'Extraordinary,' 'tremendous,' 'exhilarating,' 'magnificent': Middle School At-Risk Students Become Avid Word Learners with the Vocabulary Self-Collection Strategy (VSS)." (Ruddell and Shearer 2002)

◆   Professional Books about Vocabulary

   ◆   *Bringing Words to Life: Robust Vocabulary Instruction* (Beck, McKeown, and Kucan 2002)

   ◆   *Teaching Vocabulary to Improve Reading Comprehension* (Nagy 1988)

   ◆   *Words, Words, Words: Teaching Vocabulary in Grades 4–12* (Allen 1999)

   ◆   *The Vocabulary Book: Learning and Instruction* (Graves 2006)

## Method of Study

- The group will obtain a comprehensive collection of professional materials on vocabulary, either through the reading coach or with funds designated for professional library materials.

- The group will divide professional articles among the members as a type of jigsaw activity so everyone receives a cross-section of the available research on vocabulary.

- The group will peruse the books and determine the one (or more) that will be most helpful in meeting their students' needs.

- If possible, the group will engage a consultant to provide a workshop on effective vocabulary instructional practices.

## Actions Resulting from Learning

1. The group will form one or more study groups based on the professional book(s) related to vocabulary. See Chapter 7 for more information on the logistics of forming study groups.

2. After reflecting upon the information gleaned from all resources, the group will decide which vocabulary instructional practices will be most helpful for their students. Each member will commit to incorporating one or more new practices into their classroom instruction.

3. Group members will analyze and reflect upon vocabulary practices by engaging in one or more of the following activities.

   - Supporting each other through team-teaching or peer coaching. See Chapter 8 for information regarding peer coaching.

   - Bringing student work samples to the meeting and discussing if and how vocabulary instructional practices have improved students' vocabulary skills.

   - Reflecting in writing or through dialogue about how to deepen students' long-term vocabulary development as they become independent learners.

   - Designing projects to help students conceptualize word meanings.

   - Differentiating vocabulary instruction according to individual students' strengths and needs.

## Time Frame for Action

- One semester

## Dissemination of Learning

◆ Members will share their experiences with each other and with other members of the faculty by creating a summary of their study and providing a booklet of vocabulary instructional practices they have found to be effective.

## Assessing Action

◆ The group will collect formal and informal data to determine to what extent students' vocabulary skills have improved, such as the following:

   ◆ Standardized test scores

   ◆ Teacher-made tests

   ◆ Student writing samples

   ◆ Teacher observation

## Example 2: Learning Action Plan to Improve Literacy Instructional Practices

The LLC may determine that many students are spending too much time sitting in rows engaged in passive learning activities, such as listening to lectures, taking notes, and filling out worksheets. While members determine that they want to engage students more actively, they may not know *how* to make it happen. Many secondary teachers may identify with the comment of a high school science teacher who said, "Just tell me what to do and how to do it!" As literacy learning communities often discover, it is not quite as simple as that.

## Focus of Study

◆ Increasing instructional practices that target active, deep learning

## Goal of Learning

◆ The LLC will learn how to incorporate interactive and differentiated learning activities into their classroom instructional practices.

## Goal of Action

◆ Students will become more engaged in learning, which will lead to deeper understanding of content-area subjects.

## Resources

1. Onsite reading coach, district reading specialist, consultant with specialty in differentiated instruction, and/or teachers on staff at nearby schools who utilize collaborative learning

2. Professional Materials

   ◆ *Classroom Instruction That Works* (Marzano, Pickering, and Pollock 2001)

   ◆ *Engaging Adolescent Learners: A Guide for Content-Area Teachers* (Lent 2006)

   ◆ *Fulfilling the Promise of the Differentiated Classroom: Strategies and Tools for Responsive Teaching* (Tomlinson 2003)

   ◆ *Differentiated Instruction: A Guide for Middle and High School Teachers* (Benjamin 2003)

   ◆ *Engaging Readers and Writers with Inquiry: Promoting Deep Understandings in Language Arts and the Content Areas with Guiding Questions* (Wilhelm 2007)

   ◆ *In the Middle: New Understandings About Writing, Reading and Learning* (Atwell 1998)

   ◆ *Making Sense of History: Using High-Quality Literature and Hands-on Experiences to Build Content Knowledge* (Zarnowski 2006)

   ◆ *Socratic Circles: Fostering Critical Thinking in Middle and High Schools* (Copeland 2005)

   ◆ *Speaking Volumes: How to Get Students Discussing Books* (Gilmore 2006)

   ◆ *Subjects Matter: Every Teacher's Guide to Content-Area Reading* (Daniels and Zemelman 2004)

## Method of Study

◆ Members will each select a book from the above list to read and share with the rest of the group.

◆ Members will observe teachers and students in classrooms where they are engaged in active, differentiated learning.

◆ Members will enlist the help of a teacher or reading coach who will act as a coach/mentor.

## Actions Resulting from Learning

1.  Members will form a coteaching situation where two teachers combine their classes for the purpose of interactive learning. Following are examples of ways teachers may incorporate active learning practices into their curriculum:

    ◆ Allow students to engage in student study groups for deeper understanding of a topic instead of having them simply read the chapter and answer questions in preparation for a test. (See Chapter 10 in *Engaging Adolescent Learners* [Lent 2006] for information on how to form student study groups.)

    ◆ Have students compose a piece of writing by utilizing the workshop approach. See Atwell's *In the Middle* (1998) for information on how to set up a writing workshop.

    ◆ Have students engage in a meaningful discussion of a text where every student contributes either in a small group or with the whole class by using the Socratic Circle model. See *Socratic Circles* (Copeland 2005) for tips on creating Socratic dialogues within content-area classes. *Speaking Volumes* (Gilmore 2006) also provides activities for getting students involved in interactive learning.

    ◆ Have students engage in an inquiry approach in content-area classes through small-group projects based on brainstorming, developing a model for investigation, and presenting findings to the class. See *Engaging Readers and Writers with Inquiry* (Wilhelm 2002) for help with creating an inquiry-guided curriculum.

    ◆ Provide students with supplemental texts related to a topic and guide them in forming essential questions that they will answer through investigation of various texts. See *Making Sense of History* (Zarnowski 2006) for specific practices to engage students in active, cross-curricular learning.

2.  Members will bring videotapes of interactive classroom activities to LLC meetings for the purpose of reflection on how activities increase student learning.

3. Ask a student to become a record keeper as teachers introduce new activities—keeping handouts, noting student comments, and taking photographs as the class engages in collaborative learning. Bring notebooks to meetings as a prompt for dialogue and reflection.

## Time Frame for Action

◆ A school year

## Dissemination of Learning

1. Members will videotape classroom activities that incorporate active learning to share with members of the faculty who may be interested in trying such practices.

2. The following year, members will offer to coteach or peer-coach other members of the faculty who want to try new practices.

3. Members will place notebooks documenting the effectiveness of new interactive instructional practices in the school's professional library.

## Assessment of Action

1. The group will survey students and ask them specifically if and how their learning increased in classes that incorporated collaborative learning.

2. The group will examine attendance records and test scores of students in classes utilizing collaborative learning and compare those with similar records from previous years.

## *Example 3: Learning Action Plan to Create Schoolwide Literacy Initiative*

Often LLCs are tasked with developing a schoolwide literacy initiative or recommending a particular program for the school's intensive reading classes. Sometimes schools jump into an initiative without first studying its potential benefits and drawbacks or finding out if the research backing the program applies to the school's population. Packaged reading programs can cost hundreds of thousands of dollars, so it is especially important for the LLC to become knowledgeable before investing time or money in programs that may not be best suited for their students.

## Focus of Study

◆ The LLC will find schoolwide literacy initiatives or reading programs to meet the needs of students.

## Goal of Learning

◆ The LLC will learn which literacy initiatives or programs will work best in meeting the needs of the school's student population.

## Goal of Action

◆ The LLC will recommend a plan for the school to consider in meeting students' literacy needs.

## Resources

1. National professional organizations' policy briefs on adolescent literacy:
   - ◆ National Council of Teachers of English – "NCTE Principles of Adolescent Literacy Reform – A Policy Research Brief"
   - ◆ Alliance for Excellent Education – "A Report from Carnegie Corporation of New York: Reading Next: A Vision for Action and Research in Middle and High School Literacy"
   - ◆ Alliance for Excellent Education – "A Report to Carnegie Corporation of New York: Writing Next: Effective Strategies to Improve Writing of Adolescents in Middle and High Schools"
   - ◆ International Reading Association – "Adolescent Literacy: A Position Statement Supporting Young Adolescents' Literacy Learning: A Joint Position Statement of the International Reading Association and the Middle School Association"
   - ◆ American Institutes of Research – "Lessons and Recommendations from the Alabama Reading Initiative: Sustaining Focus on Secondary Reading"

2. Professional journal articles:
   - ◆ "Learning from What Doesn't Work" (Ivey and Fisher 2005)
   - ◆ "Youth in the Middle: Our Guides to Improved Literacy Instruction" (Alvermann 2006)

3. Professional books targeting adolescent literacy:

- *Adolescent Literacy: Turning Promise into Practice* (Beers, Probst, and Rief 2007)

- *Creating Literacy-Rich Schools for Adolescents* (Ivey and Fisher 2006)

- *Do I Really Have to Teach Reading? Content, Comprehension, Grades 6–12* (Tovani 2004)

- *Reading for Understanding: A Guide to Improving Reading in Middle and High School Classrooms* (Schoenbach et al. 1995)

- *Reading and the Middle School Student* (Irvin 1998)

- *Reading and the High School Student* (Irvin, Buehl, and Klemp 2003)

- *The Reading Zone* (Atwell 2007)

- *The SSR Handbook: How to Organize and Manage a Sustained Silent Reading Program* (Pilgreen 2001)

4. Schools with exemplary reading programs in place

5. Commercially packaged reading programs

## Method of Study

1. The group will examine a different position paper or journal article at each meeting.

2. Members of the group will choose one or more professional books on adolescent literacy to read.

3. The group will make plans to visit a school with an effective literacy initiative in place.

## Actions Resulting from Learning

1. At each meeting, members will use information from their reading to chart elements of exemplary literacy programs.

2. After members feel that they are sufficiently knowledgeable, they will examine commercially prepared literacy programs and/or develop a literacy initiative such as a content-area reading comprehension plan or school-wide independent reading (SIR) plan. Figure 6.2 shows a sample SIR plan.

## Time Frame for Action

- One semester

## Dissemination of Learning

1. Members will provide research regarding effective literacy practices to the faculty and district reading coach.

2. Members of the LLC will do book talks at faculty meetings and ask other faculty members to read young adult fiction or nonfiction books and present their reflections about the books at the next faculty meeting.

---

# Sample Plan for
# Schoolwide Independent Reading

◆ Fifteen minutes will be added to second period. Each day, at the beginning of second period, all students in all classes will read a book of their choice.

◆ Students will read at least two hundred pages each month.

◆ Student will maintain a reflective reading log. Prompts will be provided to teachers to help students get started.

◆ Students will write reflective letters about their reading when they finish each book. Letters may be addressed to a staff member, another student, an adult outside of the school, or the author.

◆ Once a week, students will be given the opportunity to talk about their books with other members of the class.

◆ Teachers will monitor students to ensure that they are reading and talk with them individually about their books.

◆ The media specialist will create "book bins" that teachers may check out as temporary classroom libraries.

◆ The LLC will investigate ways of procuring books for permanent classroom libraries through grants or other funding.

◆ The LLC will form a student literacy learning community to support the literacy initiative. Their tasks may include doing book talks on closed-circuit TV, writing book reviews for the school newspaper, or sharing book lists with teachers and students. See lists of young adult book reviews and recommendations from the International Reading Association, www.ira.org; The American Library Association, www.ala.org; or from The ALAN Review, a periodical from NCTE that publishes young adult book lists and author interviews, www.alan-ya.org/.

FIGURE 6.2

3. Members will incorporate a schoolwide (or communitywide) reading club where all faculty and students read the same book during a specified time period.

**Evaluation of Action**

◆ Standardized test scores in reading

◆ Teacher observation

◆ Student surveys regarding reading attitudes and habits before and after the reading initiative

◆ Library check-out records

◆ Photographs

The photograph in Figure 6.3 was taken at Walton Career Development Center after the school's literacy learning community devoted its time and resources to building a media center full of engaging books for their students. While the students in the Building Construction Technology class were waiting for the mortar mix, the teacher suddenly noticed that many of the students had pulled out their books and were reading. The picture is, indeed, worth a thousand words.

While the examples in this chapter may seem like rather sterile visions of a literacy learning community, the real thing will be infused with all of the excitement, energy, and collaborative commitment that the faculty at Walton Middle School experienced. It will take time, of course, for the group to learn to dance to each other's tunes and still remain in step, but soon they will be swaying as one to the music they have created.

## *Questions for Reflection*

1. What goal or goals do you have for your own learning and actions related to that learning, either personally or professionally?

2. How do you plan to accomplish those goals?

3. When you make plans for a new project or new learning, do you write out the plans? Create a calendar? Wait and see what happens?

4. How patient are you with planning before taking action?

5. Do you prefer to work alone or with a group when you embark upon new learning or a new project?

FIGURE 6.3

## Reflection Through Action

One of the best ways for a literacy learning community to begin developing a plan is for members to have extended time together. Not only do they learn to rely on each other while providing different pieces of the puzzle for their literacy plan, but they also form long-lasting relationships. Just as time outside of class in the form of field trips makes learning more authentic for students, these types of experiences also serve to ground adults' learning. Consider one or more of the following field trips:

1. Rent cottages, condominiums, or cabins in a serene place, such as in a state park or near a lake for an overnight meeting. Families may be invited to this retreat, but make sure time is allotted for the members to discuss their goals and plans.

2. Plan to go to a literacy conference together. Write a proposal to present the work you have been doing and ask for funding to pay for the trip since you will be bringing recognition to the school or district. Various national conferences occur throughout the year all over the United States. Many of the following organizations have regional or state conferences, as well.

- ALAN: Assembly on Literature for Adolescents of the National Council of Teachers of English, www.alan-ya.org

- Association for Supervision and Curriculum Development, www.ascd.org

- National Urban Alliance, www.nuatc.org

- Coalition of Essential Schools, www.essentialschools.org

- International Reading Association, www.ira.org

- National Council of Teachers of English, www.ncte.org

3. Get to know the student literacy learning community by arranging to take them on field trips to hear an author speak, participate in a writing conference, visit a museum, or see a play. Begin forming a school-wide learning community by celebrating literacy experiences whenever possible.

## *Study Group Resources: Adolescent Literacy*

- *Adolescent Literacy: Turning Promise into Practice* (Beers, Probst, and Rief 2007)

- *Engaged Reading: Processes, Practices, and Policy Implications* (Guthrie and Alvermann 1999)

- *Redefining Literacy for the Twenty-first Century* (Warlick 2004)

- *What Adolescents Deserve: A Commitment to Students' Literacy Learning* (Rycik and Irvin 2001)

*Section Three*

# Developing Tools for Literacy Learning

I lived in Master Hugh's family about seven years. During this time, I succeeded in learning to read and write. In accomplishing this, I was compelled to resort to various stratagems.

—FREDERICK DOUGLASS, *NARRATIVE OF THE LIFE OF FREDERICK DOUGLASS: AN AMERICAN SLAVE*

As the initial LLC brings the idea of collective learning to the faculty and students, they will introduce tools that will support and expand the concept of learning together. While formats, templates, and specific instructions can be found in many professional books, it is best to understand the concept behind these collaborative activities and adapt them to fit the needs of your school community. Tools are not an end in themselves; they must be utilized within an entire context of embedded staff development.

## Tools for Authentic, Embedded, Sustained Staff Development

Study Groups are small groups of people who come together to study a variety of topics for the purpose of increasing student learning. Peer coaching occurs when colleagues share their teaching by planning together, engaging in common experiences, and practicing new skills and strategies within a safe and supportive environment. Action research is a process where colleagues collect and analyze data to diagnose problems, search for solutions, take action on to explore possibilities, and monitor how well the action worked.

# Learning Through
# Study Groups

"I just like to know," said Pooh humbly.

—A.A. MILNE, *WINNIE THE POOH*

As the youngest teacher in Mowat Junior High School's English department, I was eager to make a difference with my students and hungry to learn from the other teachers with whom I worked. I couldn't have started out in a better place. The teachers in this department were immersed in professional dialogue before school, in halls during change of classes, in long learning meetings after school—and on more than one occasion during overnight retreats. I was more than a bit in awe of my colleagues—and rightly so. Many of them went on to have impressive careers both in the classroom and at the district office; and the department chair, Gloria Pipkin, later won the prestigious Courage Award for her unyielding defense of our reading program. So, I must confess that it is easy to become a part of a study group when your colleagues are knowledgeable, have a genuine desire to learn, and will willingly participate in study with you.

My first year I was assigned a seventh-grade English class and, armed with Warriner's grammar book, I relentlessly began plowing through the chapters with my students: parts of speech, verb conjugation, punctuation, and usage. I sprinkled in some writing assignments and whole-class reading selections, but it was a pretty grim deal both for me and for my students. One day, a teacher who had been reading that month's issue of

NCTE's *English Journal* commented that teaching grammar in isolation did not translate to improved writing and, worse, replaced instruction in real reading and writing. That statement was the catalyst for my initiation into study groups. I was not immediately convinced and argued that students had to know grammar to construct correct sentences, but after reading professional materials and engaging in discussions about the advantages of teaching grammar within the context of students' writing, I slowly began to alter my views. A few years later, Mowat's English department won a Center of Excellence Award from NCTE, due in large part to the ongoing study that had become a trademark of our learning community.

Over twenty years later, I found myself teaching in a high school that lacked a learning community or even a small study group. My need to fill this void led me to apply for a position at the University of Central Florida, and I was thrilled to be hired as one of a team of thirteen educators tasked with creating a literacy project that would provide professional development to teachers and administrators across Florida. It was, from the time I became a part of the initiative until I left five years later, a study in learning. The team members came from all corners of Florida to meet for days at a time on UCF's campus with our director and colearner Dr. Patricia Striplin, who reminded us often that we had to fill our own well before we could hope to fill others'. As a literacy learning community, we studied, dialogued, planned, and evaluated. Our conversations often lasted late into the night and continued through extended phone or email exchanges once we returned home. Dr. Striplin understood that funding, resources, and opportunities were only accessories to knowledge—that learning was really the only thing, in the end, that would make a difference. Thus, I began and ended my Florida Department of Education career within the warm circle of a study group.

## Forming a Study Group

We were always in dialogue with others—those who taught us to read, those for whom we wrote, who lent us books, shaped our preferences, encouraged us, forbade us even.

—MARGARET MEEK

Study groups are simply small groups of people who come together for a common purpose, learning that will directly benefit their students. In an article titled "Teacher Talk" Reggie Routman describes the specifics of a study group: "When teachers are well informed—by learning theory and relevant research, as well as by careful reflection on their own experiences—they can make confident decisions about teaching practices" (2002, 32). In addition, research has confirmed that study groups have a direct and positive impact upon student learning. Murphy and Lick, in their comprehensive book, *Whole-Faculty Study Groups,* point to student results over a period of time showing "an increase in achievement and a decrease in disruptive behavior" when their teachers participated in study groups (2001, 3). They note that study groups generate other advantages for the school as a whole, such as support and encouragement of teachers, and a sense of collective energy and synergy. Murphy and Lick believe that the greatest advantages accrue when all faculty members in the school participate in a study group. I propose that study groups should be a tool used within literacy learning communities, just as action research and coaching are tools for learning. In fact, systemic staff development through literacy learning communities *will* eventually include all members of the school—even students— but it may be a slow and gradual process.

John Dewey notes that *desire* is one of several components necessary for thoughtful, reflective learning. I have seen study groups sabotaged by a member who has absolutely no desire to be there, but must sit through the meeting because it is mandated by the principal. In one high school, the principal organized study groups during each faculty member's planning period using Kylene Beer's book *When Kids Can't Read, What Teachers Can Do* as the study group text. Some of the groups worked well and engaged in extensive conversations, bringing in student work samples as they tried out various instructional practices in their classes. Another group got hung up on who would have what role (facilitator, recorder, timekeeper) and one group relied on the reading coach to provide summaries of the chapters at each meeting. I have witnessed so many of these scenarios that I now believe that study groups should be formed in direct response to learning needs within a literacy learning community rather than mandated for all.

Schools that have established a culture of inquiry and dialogue are primed for forming study groups within the faculty, and they will spread naturally if they are one of several choices for embedded staff development. While there are many models of study groups available to schools and many sample forms to document evidence of study, the format should not dictate the learning. At Mowat Junior High, the English department fostered an environment of learning and engagement that became a systemic part of the culture. It was a large department, and those who felt uncomfortable with our "learning style" eventually left to teach in a more traditional setting. Study groups supported our work as a literacy learning community, and when the need arose to study a topic, those who were interested engaged in the study. I remember reading Peter Elbow's *Writing Without Teachers* with several other teachers and discussing his ideas for freewriting and responding to writing as a way of improving our writing practices. That year, not coincidentally, our students won almost all of the writing awards in every category in the district writing contest.

Of course, study groups have been around since Socrates' time because, as tabloid sales currently show, people *want to know.* Despite the prevalence of superficial bits of information, there is no better way to deepen learning about complex issues than with a team of people who have a genuine desire to learn. Individual thinking taps into collective learning where there is the potential for "many minds to be more intelligent than one mind," as Peter Senge describes it (1990, 236). In fact, study groups sometimes end up looking like poster children for the overused K-W-Ls as they determine what they know about a topic, identify what they want to know, and then evaluate what they have learned. Many study groups, both formal and informal, develop because inquiries prompt them to examine a topic. The following questions may help groups guide their study.

## Study Group Considerations

◆ What question or topic prompted the formation of the study group?

◆ Why do we want to know?

◆ How will our knowledge increase student learning?

◆ What will we do with our new learning?

Once members have determined the reason for the study, they should form a study group plan that fits the group's personality. The following suggestions will help schools that are beginning to incorporate this type of professional learning into their staff development.

## Study Group Logistics

Generally, study groups are composed of four to six members who will commit to a course of learning determined by a common question, interest, topic, or need. Roles may not be necessary in many groups, but some may want to delineate tasks in the following ways.

## Study Group Roles

1. The facilitator guides the discussion and makes sure each member's contributions are acknowledged. He or she should be a good listener, well organized, and skilled in working with people. The facilitator is a team builder, not a dictator and, as such, will encourage members to contribute, gain different perspectives from each other, and reflect on new learning.

2. The recorder keeps careful notes and provides copies of the notes for other members of the team after each meeting. In addition, he or she will create a notebook of artifacts, data, and study summaries as outlined in the Study Group Learning Log (Figure 7.1).

3. The timekeeper makes sure the meeting begins and ends promptly and will send out reminders of meeting dates and times.

There may be other roles based on the group's needs, such as summarizer, researcher, reporter, or even social chair, but the above three roles will ensure that the group functions efficiently. A study group may also want to create guiding principles, similar to those created by a literacy learning community. Chapter 4 contains information for developing such guidelines.

Often, administrators want documentation of ongoing professional development. The Study Group Learning Log is a way of recapping the group's learning as they make plans for their next meeting. Figure 7.1 has been adapted from *Engaging Adolescent Learners* (Lent 2006) and can be used with student study groups in the classroom as well as with adult study groups.

In an article published in the *Journal of Staff Development*, I make the case that reflection can be enriched through the practice of writing, especially within study groups. "Study groups read, discuss, and plan but sometimes overlook the importance of learning through writing" (2006, 49). I suggest that at the end of each study group session, participants should write as a way of reflecting on and assimilating what they have learned. The following are prompts to encourage individual reflection through writing.

Obviously, study groups are most successful when members have *time* to study and talk with each other. Regie Routman noted that at first the conversations in teacher study groups may be superficial because teachers aren't used to this type of learning. They "air their feelings about school life" instead of focusing on curriculum and improving student learning

## Prompts for Reflective Writing

◆ Explore an idea that surfaced in today's meeting through freewriting.

◆ What new instructional practice do you want to try in your classroom based on what you learned today?

◆ What challenges do you foresee in implementing a new practice?

◆ How would you like to change your curriculum?

◆ What is preventing you from making such a change?

◆ Write about one particular student and what you have learned from him or her.

◆ Write a conversation you would like to have with a student, another teacher, administrator, or legislator.

◆ Write an outline of an article that you could submit to a professional journal.

(2002, 3, 4). As a consultant, I meet with groups of teachers for entire days, often within departments or teams. I always begin our sessions by asking teachers to talk about classroom practices, common literacy challenges, or content-area issues. Inevitably, the first hour or so is a bit stiff because teachers are not accustomed to sitting still, facing each other, and simply talking. Instead, they are used to being "on" as one teacher noted, "from bell to bell" and rarely have time to *think*, much less time to listen as someone else responds thoughtfully. As the day progresses, however, I observe teachers settling into their new roles as participants in meaningful conversations. Questions also emerge, such as this one from a first-year social studies teacher to his colleagues, a question that later led to in-depth dialogue. "How important is it that I follow the sequence as outlined in the textbook? What if something comes up in the news that is in a chapter at the back of the book? Should I skip to that chapter to make the current event relevant to the curriculum?"

In one high school science department, we were jigsawing articles from *Educational Leadership*'s "Science in the Spotlight" issue (December 2006/January 2007) as a way of examining new ideas in the science curriculum. While sharing insights, one teacher began talking about an inquiry project in her anatomy class and how it had grown into an amazing learning experience for her students. The students worked in teams to analyze how they would treat a knee injury as described by a guest speaker. After several weeks, the guest speaker returned and the class presented

# Study Group Learning Log

Topic:                                    Date:

Text:

Facilitator:

Members Present:


Five-Minute Rewind: Facilitator and recorder review major points of discussion from last meeting.

Five-Minute Fast Forward: Facilitator reminds group of goals of study.

Group Action. Consider the following prompts when recording the actions of the group.

1. What did members read, write, or what student data did they collect to prepare for the meeting?

2. What major points did the group address in today's meeting? Summarize the content covered.

3. What new learning occurred today?

4. What questions emerged as a result of the dialogue?

5. Who will attempt to find answers to the questions?

6. What other resources (such as teachers, experts in field, professional books, or articles) will be needed to address questions for ongoing learning?

7. What will be the focus of the next meeting?

8. If additional materials or resources are needed, who will be responsible for bringing them to the next meeting?

9. What will members read or write in preparation for the next meeting?

10. Best quotes from today's meeting. Write the quotes verbatim, giving credit to the author or speaker.

Additional Notes:

FIGURE 7.1

their findings to him as if they were various medical practitioners going through the process of explaining the nature of the injury and their recommendation for treatment. While the project itself was an exciting format for learning, it was the reaction of other science teachers that interested me. One teacher said, "I didn't know about that!" She was amazed that such a powerful learning experience was happening right next door. By the end of the meeting, the department head had gained permission from the principal for a follow-up, all-day meeting to explore other inquiry projects the entire department might pursue the following year.

## Types of Study Groups

What we have learned from others becomes our own by reflection.

—RALPH WALDO EMERSON

As the initial learning community makes plans for expanding learning throughout the faculty during the second year, they may suggest various types of study groups, either as tools for learning within LLCs or as stand-alones, to help teachers in their professional learning. Following are descriptions of four specific study groups that may help you get started.

---

**Study Group 1: Study to Increase Content-Area Knowledge**
Linda Darling-Hammond points out that one of the most important functions of professional development is making sure teachers understand the subject matter they teach. "They (teachers) need to know meanings and connections, not just procedures and information" (Darling-Hammond and Sykes 1999, 7). She goes on to say that her research has shown that the single most important factor for students' success is the knowledge and skills of the teacher. Thomas Guskey, in *Evaluating Professional Development*, also confirms that curriculum workshops offer "clear, positive benefits to both teachers and students" (2000, 155).

Teachers have entered their particular field in most cases because of an affinity for or interest in the subject, so it is a natural transition for them to engage in study groups related to their content area. Some teachers may need to broaden their knowledge of issues not currently in textbooks or update their knowledge about topics that have evolved as new information is forthcoming, such as global warming, neuroplasticity, or terrorism. New teachers or teachers who have been assigned subjects they have not previously taught may also find much-needed support by participating in a study group that helps them better understand the content they are expected to teach.

One area that begs for a study group is reading, both for teachers of reading classes and for content-area teachers. There are countless resources available, such as McREL's excellent series of books about reading in various content areas, published by the Association for Supervision and Curriculum Development.

- ◆ *Teaching Reading in Science*
- ◆ *Teaching Reading in Mathematics*
- ◆ *Teaching Reading in Social Studies*
- ◆ *Teaching Reading in the Content Areas: If Not Me, Then Who?*

In addition, districts should provide time for literacy coaches to meet on a regular basis for the specific purpose of study and dialogue. The Literacy Coaching Clearinghouse (www. literacycoachingonline.org), a joint venture of The International Reading Association and National Council of Teachers of English, provides updated resources, the latest literacy research, and extensive support, all of which are raw materials for study groups. There are increasing numbers of professional books and articles on coaching as well that would make appropriate study group selections.

## Study Group 2: Study for Credit

Many diverse groups in a school or district may already be engaged in a study based on a desire or need for advanced degrees, certification, National Board documentation, or any other number of purposes. Study groups are natural vehicles for making such work less burdensome and more enjoyable. Teachers struggling with becoming "highly qualified" may find themselves becoming *supremely* qualified by sharing their knowledge with each other as they jump together through state and federal hoops.

## Study Group 3: Study Through Book Clubs

This study group is one that has the potential for bringing the school, students, and surrounding community together by offering study groups on a specific book, such as a work of award-winning fiction or a thought-provoking piece of nonfiction. For example, Nathaniel Philbrick's well-written *Mayflower* provides primary documents to support his fascinating account of the Pilgrims' famous voyage, one that may forever alter our view of how America began. Such study *is* staff development, and it has the potential to deepen knowledge in any area by tapping into supplemental texts that enrich traditional curriculum topics.

## Study Group 4: Study Related to Current Events

This study group might also include students, faculty, and community members. It is based on a common weekly reading of a national, state, or local current event from a periodical, such as *Time*, *Newsweek*, or local newspapers. The topic is decided prior to the meeting so that members are prepared to discuss, debate, and analyze what they have read. For example, in the news recently there have been reports of documents that prove that Otto Frank, Anne Frank's father, attempted to gain entry into the United States prior to going into hiding in 1942, but that he was unable to break through the State Department's restrictions. This "current event" could spark a cross-curricular study group about the political situation in the United States in 1942, paired with the reading of Anne Frank's diary. Such a study group would provide an opportunity for students to engage in dialogue where listening, responding to others' thoughts, and expressing viewpoints in an objective and respectful manner is the norm. The following presents other possible study group topics.

*(Continues)*

**Study Group Topics**
◆ School Policies (block scheduling, tardy policies, in-school suspension)
◆ Assessments (standardized, alternative, formative, summative, diagnostic)
◆ Classroom Management
◆ Twenty-first–Century Literacies
◆ Differentiated Instruction
◆ Discussion Techniques
◆ English Language Learning
◆ Cross-Curricular Study (interdisciplinary projects, team teaching initiatives)
◆ Technology in the Classroom
◆ Senior Projects
◆ Ninth-Grade Academies
◆ Book Challenges
◆ School Safety
◆ Literacy Incentive Programs
◆ Student Engagement/Motivation
◆ Service Learning
◆ Parental/Community Involvement
◆ Media Center Policies
◆ Classroom Libraries
◆ Text Sets
◆ Bibliotherapy Using Young Adult Novels
◆ Summer Reading Activities
◆ Content-Area Reading/Writing Requirements
◆ Extracurricular Literacy Offerings
◆ Literacy Electives

Clearly, there is no end to the number or types of study groups that would support literacy learning communities. A school dedicated to ongoing learning will soon discover study groups as viable options for increasing knowledge, sharing perspectives, and sparking in-depth thinking about important and relevant topics.

## Questions for Reflection

Imagine arriving at school and being told that your only task for the day was to engage in study and dialogue with a small group of colleagues.

1. Who would be in your group?

2. Where would you meet?

3. How would you decide what issue to study?

4. What books or materials would support your study?

5. How might your teaching change when you returned to the classroom?

## Reflection Through Action

Consider making your study public by offering a community forum. Students in leadership or speech classes can learn to facilitate such a forum, and content-area classes may contribute by researching a topic prior to the event. Technology students could even create flyers or handouts citing research or main points about the issue. Often, media will be interested in covering such events and local colleges, chambers of commerce, or other schools may cosponsor them.

The National Issues Forums (www.nifi.org) provides teacher's guides to high schools or middle schools that want to introduce deliberative discussions of social issues into their classrooms, along with information on how to teach facilitation skills. They also provide high-quality booklets full of research on a variety of topics, such as:

◆ Children and Family

◆ Economic Issues

◆ Education

◆ Energy and Environment

◆ Government and Politics

◆ Health and Well-Being

◆ International and Foreign Policy

## Study Group Resources: Forming Study Groups

◆ *Redefining Staff Development: A Collaborative Model for Teachers* (Robb 2000)

◆ *Teacher Study Groups: Building Community Through Dialogue and Reflection* (Birchak et al. 1998)

◆ *Whole-Faculty Study Groups: Creating Student-Based Professional Development*, 2nd ed. (Murphy and Lick 2001)

# Learning Through Peer Coaching

Behold, I do not give lectures or a little charity,
When I give I give myself.

—WALT WHITMAN, *LEAVES OF GRASS*

If someone had asked me the definition of coaching in 1992, I may have conjured up visions of Coach Hart directing a team of very large, sweating male students as they did one more set of push-ups on the high school football field during a hot August afternoon. Or I may have pictured the female tennis coach with her whistle swinging at the end of a long blue cord atop a white polo shirt that she somehow managed to keep spotlessly clean. I did not picture a coach as someone whose job it was to help me become a better teacher.

In fact, in 1992 when Ben Dykema, a social studies teacher who was teaching many of the same students I was teaching in English, approached me with an idea for forming a team-teaching class, I never even considered the word *coaching*. The class we created, however, became a peer-coaching model, even though we didn't have a whistle between us. We began the experiment by combining his American government students and my English students. The students received two credits for a yearlong ninety-minute class, a simple adaptation of the block schedule. It was a large class, but that format created an enthusiastic community of learners that became one of the most enjoyable and productive teaching experiences of my life, an initiative that continued for over six years with a variety of classes. Although initially we decided to divide the instruction time roughly in half during the daily class period, we soon found that our styles merged seamlessly as we cotaught. *Time* magazine became our primary text for reading and writing as well as for discussions, vocabulary, and projects requiring analysis, critical thinking, and creativity. The topics changed each week, but we inevitably found articles that would merge our subjects into interdisciplinary studies. Although many years have passed since those days, students continue to contact us and reinforce our belief that this unique experience left them with in-depth understanding about many topics.

The students weren't the only ones learning in these classes. My skills as a teacher, as well as my content knowledge, increased dramatically during this time. Because Ben was always in the room when I taught, he acted as a mirror that allowed me to better understand myself as a teacher. He helped me figure out why something didn't work or why the students responded in a certain way—and I learned by simply watching him interact with the class. Because we had different strengths, we were able to expand and refine our individual teaching skills. We planned together, discussed student needs and behaviors that we both observed, experimented with new and innovative teaching practices, and learned together in an environment that invited and encouraged academic risk taking.

It wasn't until ten years later, as a member of the literacy team at the University of Central Florida, that I first heard the term *coaching* used in a way that was not tied to sports. Susan Kelly, a colleague who was to become a valuable coach and friend in my personal and professional life, identified herself as a literacy coach when I first met her. As she described her role, I recognized that Ben and I, too, had been coaches in the truest sense of the word.

When I think back on our team-teaching experience, I realize that Cambourne's Conditions of Learning are also conditions of teaching.

- *Immersion*   We, along with our students, were immersed in experiences requiring reading, writing, speaking, and listening.

- *Demonstration*   We modeled effective teaching practices to each other.

- *Expectations*   We had high expectations that this experimental class would be successful.

- *Responsibility*   We were permitted to make decisions and take responsibility about "when, how, and what" to teach within our respective curriculums.

◆ *Approximation* We were free to take risks, make mistakes, and learn from those mistakes.

◆ *Use* We used and practiced our learning in relevant settings while doing authentic tasks.

◆ *Response* We received relevant, appropriate, timely, and nonthreatening feedback in the form of authentic dialogue with each other.

Although literacy coaches are now a mainstay in most districts across the United States, the term still is not clearly defined. I recently met with a group of school-based coaches and found that, while they were doing an exemplary job of supporting teachers in their literacy endeavors by providing research and technical support as well as modeling effective practices, they had not yet developed peer-coaching relationships.

There are several different types of coaching, but the one that best supports the work of literacy learning communities is peer coaching, where colleagues share their teaching by planning together, engaging in common experiences, and practicing new skills and strategies within a safe and supportive environment. Joyce and Showers, whose work is seminal in educational coaching, provide overwhelming evidence that coaching is an effective practice. In fact, coached teachers are much more likely to use their new knowledge in classroom settings, leading directly to increased student learning, than teachers who have not had the advantage of being supported by a coach. Joyce and Showers also demonstrate the importance of peer coaching in improving student learning by citing a study where "members of peer-coaching groups exhibited greater long-term retention of new strategies and more appropriate use of new teaching models over time" (2002, 13). Their research shows, however, that offering advice to teachers following observations is not the best way to affect students' learning.

Interestingly, Joyce and Showers found that it is important to omit feedback, as traditionally defined, as a coaching component. While this may sound antithetical to the concept of coaching, they maintain that when teachers attempt to give one another conventional feedback, collaborative activity disintegrates and evaluative comments follow. Our profession has been reared on the model of observations as precursors to "feedback," frequently beginning with the phrase, "This is what you did well" right before the switch of constructive criticism stings our legs.

As I think about my team-teaching experience with Ben, I realize that our "feedback" took place in the form of conversations when we would discuss an issue that had come up during class. There was no need to ask Ben to observe my teaching for the purpose of providing feedback; our dialogue was a natural part of our professional relationship on a daily basis grounded in respect and a mutual desire to help our students learn. When I recall other coaching scenarios, such as my experience as a first-year teacher in Mowat's exemplary English department, I again realize there was no formal feedback. I learned by engaging in deep dialogue with other teachers, observing them in action, and then trying out my newfound learning in the classroom. Often, the only feedback I received was a colleague's attempt to answer my questions.

Joyce and Showers tell us they eventually needed to redefine the meaning of "coach." When pairs of teachers observed each other, they began to view the one teaching as the "coach" and the one observing as the "coached." Teachers who are observing do so in order to learn from their colleague. They point out that feedback may be in the form of brief conversations, such as, "Thanks for letting me watch you work" (1996, 14). While seeming to narrow the concept of "coach," they have actually broadened the definition by viewing peer coaching as more than observations and conferences.

Jim Knight, author of *Instructional Coaching: A Partnership Approach to Improving Instruction*, references a 1997 study where teachers reported that they were four times more likely to implement teaching practices in their classrooms when they learned in partnership situations than if they learned those same practices in traditional professional development settings. Partnership is a friendly term that gets at the heart of collaboration, perhaps even more than the coaching metaphor that implies one is an "expert" leading another to develop more expertise by following his or her sage advice.

Knight's five characteristics of partnerships reinforce both Joyce and Shower's work on peer coaching and Cambourne's Conditions of Learning.

- ◆ Professional developers and teachers are equal partners.

- ◆ Teachers should have choices regarding what and how they learn.

- ◆ Teachers should reflect and apply learning to their real-life practice as they are learning.

- ◆ Professional development should enable authentic dialogue.

- ◆ Professional development should respect and enable the voices of teachers to be heard. (2007, 27)

Peer coaching should be a partnership that is inherent in every literacy learning community as teachers cycle from being learners to practitioners and back to being learners. A school must be committed to peer coaching, however, or it will not reap its benefits. One high school attempted what they termed a team-teaching situation for an English and social studies teacher. Each teacher was assigned a full class, but in the middle of the period the students physically moved from one teacher's room to the team-teacher's room. The original idea was that the teachers would collaborate and bring students together to team-teach when appropriate. Originally, the teachers were to have a common planning period for the purpose of working together, but as is often the case, the master schedule overruled the plan. The initiative ultimately provided few advantages other than giving students a chance to stretch their legs by walking down the hall to another classroom in the middle of the period.

In providing peer coaching opportunities, especially within literacy learning communities, the school should be open to all types of collaborative relationships, especially as LLCs move into the second year. Peer coaching is a concept, not a formula, and should be based on personalities, common interests, and symbiotic relationships. Because teaching is a human endeavor, peer coaching must include all the elements of any good friendship, such as trust, compatibility, and caring. Our roles as peer coaches are not to solve problems or give advice; they are, instead, as Palmer notes in *The Courage to Teach*, an opportunity to create a conversation that "works like a navigator's triangulation, allowing us to locate ourselves more precisely on teaching's inner terrain by noting the position of others—without anyone being told that he or she should move to a new location" (1998, 147).

Although the new professional development rhetoric includes coaching as a necessary tool for school improvement, in many cases the reality behind the rhetoric still lacks the honest and uncertain components necessary to make it successful. Many administrators instruct coaches to formalize the process by filling out observation sheets or providing documented solutions to teachers' problems instead of helping teachers develop less prescribed but more relevant learning partnerships. Peer coaching should be like going back to the playground when you were a child and engaging in the types of spontaneous conversations with your friends that fed your soul, released your creativity, and helped you discover yourself so that you could become who you were meant to be. We managed to help each other grow without development plans or rubrics for feedback.

Many teachers not sold on the idea of a formal study group or not ready to engage in a literacy learning community may be willing to take the more comfortable step of forming a partnership with another teacher for the purpose of trying new practices, engaging in study, or collaborating in some other way. Chances are that many teachers have already formed coaching partnerships but are not receiving the affirmation, time, or support for the practice to reach its potential in helping students learn.

Toward the end of my classroom experience, while I was teaching English in a high school, another teacher whom I had known for many years moved into the classroom next to mine. Our philosophies concerning teaching and students were similar, but rather far removed from that of many of the other teachers in that traditional department. I was excited to have her nearby because she had been using the writing workshop approach with students, and I was anxious to learn how to incorporate it in my own classes. I could reciprocate because I had written a grant for a class subscription of current events magazines, and my friend wanted to learn how to use the magazines with her students to help them develop their critical thinking abilities. In addition, we both had extensive classroom libraries and made our libraries available to each other's students to widen their choices. We even asked the administration to install a door between our classes to make it easier to share resources and allow a more natural flow of students from one class to the next—but it didn't happen.

Nevertheless, we spent hours talking about reading, writing, and the best ways to deal with whatever challenge happened to be visiting us that day. The following year, we asked for common planning periods, but again, it didn't happen. It is clear to me now, looking back, that we were attempting to create a peer-coaching situation to enrich and expand our learning, even though at the time we often felt that we were acting like kids who were socializing too much in class. If only we had been aware of Joyce and Showers' research then. We could have shown our principal how our collaboration would increase student learning, and we may have been able to convince him that our professional partnership was one he should have encouraged and supported.

## Peer Coaching as Collaboration

> Collaborate comes from "co-labor." Collaboration involves people with different resources working together as equals to achieve goals.
>
> —Arthur Costa and Robert Garmston, *Cognitive Coaching*

One of the reasons that teachers are reluctant to engage in partnerships is because the structure of schools sometimes makes it difficult to do so.

Timed learning segments and the notion that a certain curriculum belongs exclusively to a specific department (or teacher) divides a faculty and invites fragmentation in place of unity. This atmosphere can be softened by talking openly about ways in which the faculty can embrace the concept of peer coaching. If asked, teachers may think of innovative ways to partner, such as the following.

## Examples of Peer Coaching

1. Those who teach two different subjects but share the same students may engage in cross-curricular study or common thematic units. For example, they may

   ◆ combine the study of the Vietnam War from a historical perspective in social studies with its study through literature in English

   ◆ combine a reading class and math class to utilize strategies for problem solving and vocabulary study

   ◆ combine a technology class with an art class to create graphic projects

   ◆ combine a psychology class with a PE class for the purpose of gathering data on motivation for winning in sports

2. Teachers in the same content area may peer-coach as they experiment with a new practice, such as

   ◆ literature circles or student study groups

   ◆ inquiry-based research projects

   ◆ content-area study using supplemental texts or primary documents

   ◆ classroom management procedures

   ◆ discussion techniques

   ◆ alternative assessment

3. Teachers who are interested in learning about a different content-area subject or want to broaden their knowledge in their own content area may team-teach in the following ways:

   ◆ A chemistry teacher who has never taught biology may coteach with a biology teacher who has never taught chemistry.

   ◆ An English teacher with an interest in poetry may coteach with an English teacher wishing to infuse the study of literature with poetry.

♦ A teacher who uses multiple intelligences or varying learning styles in instructional practices may coteach with a teacher who wants to incorporate the practice.

4. Teachers interested in experimenting with project-based or service learning might collaborate in the following ways:

♦ Two science teachers may combine their classes to build a greenhouse or create a composting project.

♦ A ninth-grade and senior English teacher may partner in creating freshman and senior projects.

♦ A guidance counselor and child development teacher may work together to create a program in which their students mentor children in a nearby elementary school.

5. Teachers with common goals or those who teach a common course may want to develop materials they can share; for example,

♦ a lab experiment for teaching a common science concept

♦ a strategy for activating background knowledge about new topics

♦ a booklet of graphic organizers for use in history classes

♦ a variety of writing assignments for a young adult novel

## *Creating a Peer-Coaching Environment*

I have come to depend on those places where I live and work.

—BARBARA KINGSOLVER, *SMALL WONDER*

A middle school found funding to provide teachers with a substitute for a day so they could engage in professional development. There had been no dialogue about learning communities, peer coaching, or collaborative activities in this school, so many teachers spent their day sitting alone in workrooms grading papers. While this opportunity provided teachers with much-needed time to get caught up, their actions probably did little to increase student learning.

Like other systemic professional development initiatives, peer coaching will rarely happen on its own and must be supported by the principal and the school's infrastructure, even if it means creating smaller schools within schools or content-area academies, or scattering the master schedule to the wind and starting over. Teachers who commit to peer coaching should be given every opportunity to work together as they share the responsibility for professional learning.

## Supporting Peer Coaching

◆ Allow teachers to change rooms to be in closer proximity to those with whom they wish to partner.

◆ Set up a space in the school with professional books and journals, comfortable chairs, library tables, and good lighting. This should be a space where study and dialogue in a professional and quiet setting are supported, a place other than the faculty workroom.

◆ Provide rooms that are large enough to hold more than one group of students at a time for teachers who want to combine classes for projects or team-teaching activities. For example, open up the cafeteria before or after lunch for class use.

◆ Keep inservice days free to allow teachers extended time for planning with a partner. Provide stipends for teachers who want to collaborate during the summer.

◆ Provide time during faculty meetings for partners to meet. Exclude them from other professional development activities as a way of valuing the important work they are doing together.

◆ Allow partners to attend conferences together or visit other schools if the experience will advance their targeted professional development goals.

Once teachers experience the benefits of peer coaching, they will be more likely to experiment with various formats and seek out others on the faculty with whom they may partner. Legitimize the relationship by asking them to complete a Peer Coaching Contract, such as the one in Figure 8.1.

In this time of high-stakes accountability, relationships in schools have given way to isolationism and competition, but the human dynamics of learning and teaching will not survive the coldness of those elements. Despite the popularity of scientifically based learning, one-size-fits-all strategies, and a room full of data, we must be in relationships with each other to achieve our greatest potential — and we must model those relationships to our students. Synergy, collaboration, and collegiality are simply tags that make professional development sound like it is doing its job, but the words have no power unless we are committed to bringing them to life.

# Peer Coaching Contract

Peer Coaching Partners

Describe the purpose of your collaboration.

Describe how you will work together.

List the resources or materials that will support your work.

Describe how you will accomplish the logistical arrangements. For example, in what way might your collaboration involve changing physical space, moving students, altering the schedule, etc.?

How will you evaluate the effectiveness of your peer coaching initiative?

Additional Comments:

FIGURE 8.1

## Questions for Reflection

1. Think about a project, perhaps in college or around the house, when a friend helped you with the task.

2. How would the experience have been different if you had engaged in the task alone?

3. Think about your experience when you first began teaching or during a practicum. In what way did another teacher or administrator help you?

4. Think about a time when you coached a student, either in sports or in the classroom. How did that experience differ from "teaching" him or her?

## Reflection Through Action

Peer coaching is a practice that will be as beneficial to students as it is to adults. Teaching students how to work together in a respectful and supportive way will enhance their emotional quotient as well as their academic skills and will provide them with important learning they will rely on throughout life.

Consider starting a student peer-coaching initiative throughout the school or in your own class. While it will take some time for students to become accustomed to this type of learning, they will soon adapt the skills to all content area classes. Chapter 12 in *Engaging Adolescent Learners* (Lent 2006) offers a detailed plan for incorporating student peer coaching into the school culture. In the meantime, place students in pairs and have them help each other with an assignment by following a format similar to the one that follows.

## Instructions for Student Peer Coaches

1. Provide students with a challenging content-related task, such as solving a difficult problem in math or responding to a poem that may be hard to comprehend.
2. Allow students to choose a peer coach with whom they want to work.
3. Have them use the following prompts to coach each other through the task.
   ◆ What is it you don't understand?
   ◆ How would you approach this part of the problem, poem, or task?
   ◆ Let's talk through how you might comprehend this.
   ◆ Have you had difficulties with this type of assignment in the past? How did you figure it out?
   ◆ Should we ask (the teacher, another student, a parent) for help with this?
   ◆ Are there any resources we could use to help us?

## Study Group Resources: Peer Coaching

◆ *Cognitive Coaching: A Foundation for Renaissance Schools* (Costa and Garmston 2002)

◆ *Instructional Coaching: A Partnership Approach to Improving Instruction* (Knight 2007)

◆ *The Literacy Coach: Guiding in the Right Direction* (Puig and Froelich 2007)

◆ *Student Achievement Through Staff Development*, 3rd ed. (Joyce and Showers 2002)

# Learning Through
# Action Research

I need to forge relationships with my students that are
centered around books: What is this one reading?
Why, and how? How do I help her move forward?

—NANCIE ATWELL, *THE READING ZONE*

My friend Susan Kelly called one day while I was making dinner
with a question that would take more than a few minutes' conversation to address. "What if," she began as she often does,
"visualizing is a skill that doesn't *lead to* comprehension but *is a result of*
comprehension?"

"Hmm . . ." I said, intrigued, as I continued to stir spaghetti sauce.

"I mean, if I read something I didn't understand and someone told me
that it would help if I would just visualize it, *how* would that help? Don't
I have to comprehend first in order to visualize?" Susan is taking a gradu-
ate course under Dr. Zhihui Fang at the University of Florida and he had
posed the question to her earlier. Susan, now in her fully obsessive mode,
couldn't get it out of her head. "So," she continued, "all of the modeling we
are doing on visualizing may not be helping kids comprehend at all. They
have to have the vocabulary and background knowledge for sure, but visu-
alization can't increase comprehension when kids don't understand what
they are reading."

If you want to continue this conversation, I'll pass along Susan's phone
number, because I have no doubt that she is probably still involved in some
type of action research in pursuit of an answer, even as you read this.
Susan is the epitome of an action research project. She sees question

marks in everything and wants to know *how*, *why*, and *what if* long after I have decided that I just can't think about it any longer.

When she and I began working together at the University of Central Florida, we developed an action research module that we presented to teachers and administrators who were interested in the process. We tried to demystify action research by giving personal examples about how action research works for us in our daily lives. Susan and I eventually created this kind of hokey scene. In the middle of the presentation, I would pretend that I was suddenly sick, almost fall into a chair, and put my head on a table while Susan and the participants asked me questions to find out what was wrong. The last time we did this, the sponsor of the event tried to carry me out of the room, so we've had to revise our scenario, but you get the idea. As the teachers brainstormed possible reasons for my illness, we decided that if the doctor hastily diagnosed my condition as, say, an ulcer after asking only a few questions and not collecting additional information, she may prescribe medication that would harm me if I had the flu or I was pregnant (God forbid). Our point was that it is important to use many different pieces of information, often called triangulating data, to make reasonable assessments about the nature of a problem. Within such a context, action research seems the only natural way to solve problems, from finding out which of your dogs chewed on your sofa to figuring out if the Accelerated Reader program improves students' comprehension.

Action research is an important tool for LLCs as they develop literacy plans and expand their work into years two and three. While it is easy to make broad-brush statements—like my favorite truism, "Reading is the best way to improve kids' reading skills"—anyone who has been in a class with students who refuse to read may demand to know just how students' reading will improve if they won't even look at the words on the page. In another recent conversation with Susan, she illustrated this point by telling me that she was working with a high school teacher who was having difficulty getting her students to read. Susan has had success using text sets to engage reluctant readers, so after getting to know the students, many of whom are ELL students, she decided to introduce the topic of immigration. She said they had a great class discussion and the kids seemed ready to read, write, and talk about the topic. Susan brought in several different young adult novels for the students to peruse and asked them individually to record their first, second, and third choice. She was able to ensure that each student ended up with a "first choice" book. Initially, things went pretty well, but by the time Susan called me a few days later, she sounded frustrated and disappointed. "Now the kids are saying they don't like their books. They actually wanted to do round-robin reading, probably because it's easier. They say that they can't stay focused, because their books are boring, even though they chose the books . . ." she drifted off into a sigh. She was soon back into research mode, however, as I knew she would be, as she asked, "*Why* are they bored with reading?" We began to formulate several hypotheses.

- The students simply have difficulty with reading skills (although Susan said she didn't think that was the case based upon hearing some of them read orally).

- The students may lack sufficient background information or vocabulary to engage in the text.

- As soon as students encounter a part of the book that seems boring to them, they drift off and lose interest entirely.

- Many students have never had the experience of reading an entire book and finding joy and fulfillment in that activity, so their attitudes about reading are sabotaging their efforts at reading.

- The students aren't used to persevering at something that is difficult for them. They have trained their teachers to give in to demands to make the task easier, such as round-robin reading.

- The topic doesn't really interest the students, even though it might have initially interested them.

- The students are fully literate in other ways, such as with digital literacy, but the type of reading we are asking them to do in school doesn't require that they use their skills in relevant ways.

- The students have different expectations for a reading class—that the reading will be interesting or fun. If they were given this type of experience in another class, history, for example, where they are expected to read a textbook and answer questions, they may be more engaged and persistent.

We realized, of course, that we needed more information to determine which hypothesis, if any, was close to the target. Before we hung up, Susan was making plans for surveying the students to determine their attitudes toward reading as well as their past literacy experiences. She was also planning to have each student read aloud to her privately in an effort to determine what types of reading problems they may be having. Susan pointed out that she had little time to waste; if she continued to guess why these students were unengaged, rather than use data that would provide a definitive answer, the year would come to an end before she "got it right."

Action research, like all learning, is an ongoing process that ebbs and flows with the subject, the students, the available data, the opportunities to gather additional information, and the time allocated for reflection and analysis. But it is never really finished; one conclusion often leads to infinitely more questions, and one accomplishment may lead to a whirlwind of activity. Action research is a way of work that has always been integral to the notion of good teaching.

One of the reasons I love Parker Palmer's book *The Courage to Teach* is that he acknowledges that teaching is an endeavor that can change from moment to moment, and he affirms the difficulties inherent in every teacher's day. As he relates in the introduction

> I am a teacher at heart, and there are moments in the classroom when I can hardly hold the joy. When my students and I discover uncharted territory to explore, when the pathway out of a thicket opens up before us, when our experience is illumined by the lightning-life of the mind—then teaching is the finest work I know.
>
> But at other moments, the classroom is so lifeless or painful or confused—and I am so powerless to do anything about it—that my claim to be a teacher seems a transparent sham. (1998, 1)

Like Parker Palmer, we as teachers have all lived this paradox, and it is for all of the reasons he notes that action research is necessary. We must attempt to discover why those moments exist when we can "hardly hold the joy" or why some days in the classroom are "lifeless or painful." It is not enough to admit that that's the way it is; we must seek to know *why*.

## Defining Action Research

The truth dazzles gradually or else the world would be blind.

—EMILY DICKINSON

Emily Calhoun outlines three approaches to action research, individual, collaborative, and schoolwide, each of which utilizes collective problem solving for delving into the process of inquiry. Her definition of action research is simple and to the point: "The process allows [teachers, principals, and district office personnel] to experience problem solving and to model it for their students. They carefully collect data to diagnose problems, search for solutions, take action on promising possibilities, and monitor whether and how well the action worked" (1993, 13).

## Three Types of Action Research

◆ Individual Teacher Research focuses on change within a single classroom. One teacher may want to focus on a specific problem, such as class
management, student motivation, or reading ability. Susan's observations about the students in the high school reading class and her subse-
quent data collection will be a type of individual action research, unless
she solicits the help of other teachers who may be having the same problems. If so, the project may turn into collaborative action research.

◆ Collaborative Action Research will probably be the focus of LLCs as they
examine problems within classrooms, departments, or the school as a
whole. They may even tackle a districtwide issue that has an effect on
student learning, such as mandatory use of a certain reading program.

◆ Schoolwide Action Research may occur after LLCs have become the
norm for staff development. In this process, the school faculty selects a
problem that is systemic to the school as a whole and then collects, or-
ganizes, and interprets data. A perfect example of schoolwide action research occurred when a high school that was losing their students to a
newer school nearby examined how they might attract students to keep
the school from going into decline. They surveyed students and parents
about their educational needs and interests, and determined that establishing a variety of academies – for example, law, art, drama, and
dance – would provide specialized curriculums that would attract students from other areas of town and, possibly, keep their school doors
open. They collected data from other schools around the country that
had created academies similar to the ones they were hoping to form
and elicited help from outside sources for funding. The resulting in-
school academies, based on a schoolwide action research project, revitalized the school.

## Sagor's Action Research

Richard Sagor, in *How to Conduct Collaborative Action Research*, outlines
one process for action research. There are several methods, of course, and
the challenge lies in finding the best way to conduct research that will
meet the individual needs of your students and faculty. Sagor's five-step
process is good for those who are first engaging in action research, as it is
clear and concise.

- Problem Formulation

- Data Collection

- Data Analysis

- Reporting of Results

- Action Planning

**Problem Formulation**   Teachers identify what they know about a given problem and begin to formulate what Sagor calls Research Problem Statements. These statements clearly identify the problem in order to focus the research and data collection. It is often helpful to brainstorm all aspects of the problem first in order to create a panoramic view of it. Then, the research problem statements can be more precisely articulated. Following is an example of how a middle school's LLC might develop research-problem statements leading directly to their research questions.

- Students at Compass Middle School appear to lack the social skills required to successfully engage in group learning activities.

- We (the LLC) believe that students have had limited occasions to interact with each other in academic settings and thus have not had opportunities to learn and practice the skills necessary for collaborative learning.

- We believe that students' learning will increase if they have the opportunity to engage in group learning.

- Research Questions

  1.  What specific skills do students need to help them become successful with group learning?

  2.  Will staff development on differentiated instruction and grouping help teachers facilitate collaborative learning?

**Data Collection**   Sagor points out that "the credibility of any research effort lives or dies on the quality of the data used to support its conclusions" (1992, 10). Schools are data rich; that is, they usually contain most of the data that researchers need, both quantitative and qualitative data. See page 69 for a list of data sources that will be helpful in conducting action research. For the example regarding Compass Middle School, the LLC may collect the following data:

- Teacher observation notes about student behaviors during group work and while working individually

- Videotapes of students working in groups

- Time-on-task analysis

- Checklists of behaviors, procedures, and interactions of students in group work

- Student surveys about their attitudes toward group work

- Interviews with feeder school faculty to determine the type and extent of past collaborative learning that students experienced in earlier grades

- Student work samples (notebooks, writing samples, learning logs, oral presentations) from group as well as individual tasks

- Teacher surveys regarding their attitudes toward group work

**Data Analysis** Sagor notes, "If data collection is the heart of the research process, then data analysis is its soul" (1992, 11). At this stage, teachers look at the data to see if they can identify any trends, patterns, insights, or new understandings. Data analysis can sometimes be a tedious process that may result in researchers getting lost in small details, much like magnifying one part of a painting and becoming so intrigued with the patterns and colors they forget that without the context, this small corner has little or no meaning. Teachers need each other to sift through what they've found and fit the pieces together in a unified whole.

In our middle school example, the data may reveal that students do not have the experience or understanding to engage successfully in group work. The LLC may find that students had few opportunities for collaboration in earlier grades unless it was strictly monitored by the teacher and accompanied with specific, prescribed tasks. The student surveys may reveal that students see group learning as "free time," since they are being given choices about what and how they will learn. Although the data may show that students don't know how to learn with others in a cooperative setting, researchers may also find that middle school teachers haven't had much experience with the logistics of grouping, either, since most of their own schooling was targeted toward helping them gain expertise in their content areas.

**Reporting Results**   As the LLCs begin to draw conclusions about what they discovered from their data, it is important for them to share their findings with the entire faculty. The group of researchers should keep a notebook with the topic clearly displayed that contains data, analysis, conclusions, and the process for each action research topic. The notebooks should be placed in the professional library to help teachers in the future who may encounter these same difficulties with their students. If all LLCs document their work in such a way, the professional library will contain a rich resource of data that is customized to the school and its population of students.

**Action Planning**   If data collection and analysis are the heart and soul, then action planning brings the process to life. This exciting part of action research is where teachers make a plan based upon the information they have gleaned. With a solid understanding of the behaviors, skills, and attitudes of the students in *their own school*, the LLC is ready to develop a plan of action that will address the issue head-on. At this point, there may be some discussion about the best plan of action, but everyone agrees that the action will be based on the analysis of the data the group has collected. In the Compass Middle School example, teachers may decide that they will study professional materials about flexible grouping and differentiated instruction. They will then develop a method for slowly incorporating collaborative learning into classes by having students set ground rules for group work. Teachers will scaffold instruction in group work, perhaps utilizing fishbowl activities to help students learn what is expected from them. The group may also set up a schedule so teachers can observe each other's students as they engage in group work, helping teachers better understand the dynamics of students as they work together.

Finally, the group should evaluate their plan to determine its effectiveness in helping students become successful at collaborative learning.

> If it is true that we cannot blindly accept teaching methods touted as "best," how do we know which daily practices to question?
>
> —Maja Wilson, *Rethinking Rubrics in Writing Assessment*

While concrete plans for action research are helpful in organizing the process, action research is really just a way of thinking, an understanding that we have more questions than answers, a belief that each day we come closer to gaining one small bit of insight we are ahead of where we were yesterday. Maja Wilson modeled action research in her book *Rethinking Rubrics in Writing Assessment*, a wonderfully provocative work that allows the reader to follow her line of thinking as she collects and analyzes student data and then forms a plan of action for moving students out of a rubric straightjacket into the creative and thoughtful process of expressing themselves through the written word. Near the end of the book, after almost a hundred pages, Wilson asks, "How will we help students to wield words in ways that unleash the magnificent, transformative power of language?" (2006, 98). I suspect she asks that question each day she walks into her classroom and, like Susan Kelly, Nancie Atwell, and countless other teacher researchers, she will probably never be satisfied with the answer.

## Questions for Reflection

1.  What instructional practices do you question? Why?

2.  What parts of the curriculum do you question? Why?

3.  Are you puzzled about a particular student's learning ability? In what way?

4.  What question do you most often have when you leave school at the end of the day?

5.  If you could take a yearlong sabbatical, what would you study?

## Reflection Through Action

A small group of teachers may wish to engage in a different type of research called Lesson Study, a professional development process used in Japan similar to the action research process common in the United States. In this format, teachers examine their practice to answer questions about how they can increase their students' learning by selecting an overarching goal and related research question they want to explore. They then work collaboratively on creating "study lessons" where they draw up a detailed plan for the lesson. One of the teachers uses the lesson in a real classroom as other members observe. The group comes back together to discuss their observations. They may revise the lesson for another teacher to use while group members again observe, or a different teacher may use the original lesson in her classroom as members to gain additional insights. Teachers produce a report outlining what their study lessons have taught them with respect to their research question. Descriptions and examples of the lesson study concept are available at www.tc.columbia.edu/lessonstudy/lessonstudy.html. The March 2002 issue of *Educational Leadership* also contains an article by Tad Watanabe, titled "Learning from Japanese Lesson Study."

## Study Group Resources: Action Research

◆ *Action Research: An Educational Leader's Guide to School Improvement*, 2nd ed. (Glanz 2003)

◆ *Guiding School Improvement with Action Research* (Sagor 2000)

◆ *How to Conduct Collaborative Action Research* (Sagor 1992)

◆ *Systems for Change in Literacy Education: A Guide to Professional Development* (Lyons and Pinnell 2001)

# Epilogue:
# The Unbroken Circle

Circles create soothing space, where
even reticent people can realize
that their voice is welcome.

—MARGARET WHEATLEY

I have been accused of being overly optimistic when I describe what I believe is possible within a community of learners in schools. Perhaps it is because of my positive associations with schools, from first grade, when I really did trudge through the snow to reach the warm world of Dick and Jane, until today, when I step onto unfamiliar campuses and see students gathered in groups outside the classroom doors, seizing just one last moment of freedom before sliding into their desks. Perhaps it is because I believe, as politicians are fond of saying, we really can do better, and I'm not talking about doing better at increasing test scores. I'm talking about doing a better job of taking care of each other and relying on the only thing we can really count on—our relationships, no matter how unpredictable or complex our quirks, foibles, and delights.

The truth is that some days my optimism dims to a mere flicker as I see teachers drawing their last breath under the load of forms, mandates, testing, and someone else's definition of progress. I want to hold them in place when they talk about leaving the profession, not because they don't love

**131**

their jobs or their students but because they must fill their lungs once again. I'll admit that it scares me when I see students sleeping in class, and I observe teachers trying so hard to keep their interest. I feel alarmed and disturbed when students are denied opportunities to study art, music, or other subjects that reflect the essence of their humanness. I wonder what we are *thinking* when we stage a huge celebration for those who score well on a single test, one that overshadows the other amazing accomplishments of our students.

It seems to me that there is a proverbial elephant in the living room. We keep walking around it, putting back the knickknacks its trunk has swept off the coffee table, and hoping it won't become too restless while we are going about our day. Sometimes it seems that we are waiting for someone else to recognize the giant beast and find a way to lead it peacefully out of the front door when, in fact, it's our house, our students, and our future at stake if we don't do more than acknowledge that something has gone wrong.

While I can't pretend to know how to solve the problems of an entire education system, I do believe the research that shows that the further we stray from relationships, the less hope we have of ensuring that schools are places where students will find knowledge *and* community. The unbroken circle, then, evolves within the unique and ever-changing environment of classrooms, schools, and districts. It is a circle infused with collaboration, trust, and honest dialogue; and those in charge must keep it strong by allowing time for these fundamental elements to thrive. The circle will remain in place, although the people will inevitably change, because each new group will also be afforded opportunities to meet their students' needs by examining data other than that which appears in columns of figures. Within that circle will spin smaller spheres containing tools necessary for progress: study groups, coaching, and action research. And, the actions taken by all members of the school community – parents, students, teachers, administrators, and support staff – will address the fundamental questions of literacy.

There is no end if you believe in circles, but there is a beginning, a point at which the school will make a commitment to ongoing learning, a shared purpose, and increased understanding of ourselves, our colleagues and, most important, our students.

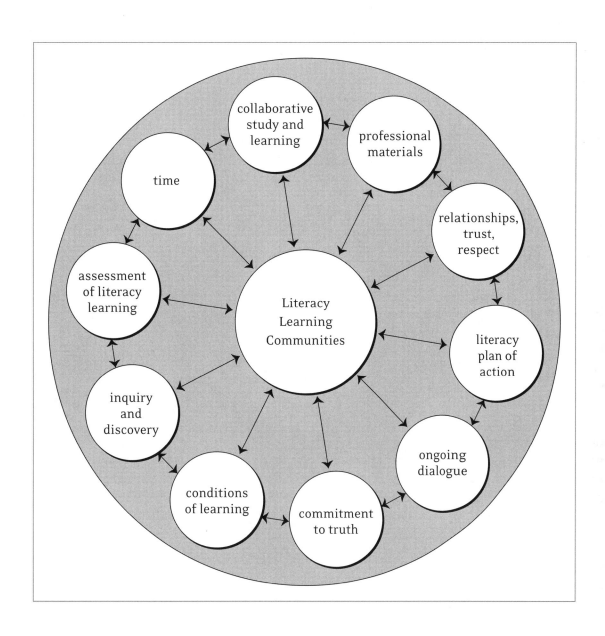

# References

ALLEN, JANET. 1999. *Words, Words, Words: Teaching Vocabulary in Grades 4–12.* Portland, ME: Stenhouse.

ALVERMANN, DONNA. 2006. "Youth in the Middle: Our Guides to Improved Literacy Instruction." *Voices from the Middle* 14 (2): 7-13.

ANDERSON, M. T. 2002. *Feed.* Cambridge, MA: Candlewick.

ATWELL, NANCIE. 1998. *In the Middle: New Understandings About Writing, Reading, and Learning.* Portsmouth, NH: Heinemann.

———. 2007. *The Reading Zone: How to Help Kids Become Skilled, Passionate, Habitual, Critical Readers.* New York: Scholastic.

BACERVICH, AMY, and TERRY SALINGER. 2006. *Lessons and Recommendations from The Alabama Reading Initiative: Sustaining Focus on Secondary Reading.* New York: Carnegie Corporation.

BARTON, MARY LEE. 2001. *Teaching Reading in Science.* Alexandria, VA: Association for Supervision and Curriculum Development.

BECK, ISABEL, MARGARET MCKEOWN, and LINDA KUCAN. 2002. *Bringing Words to Life: Robust Vocabulary Instruction.* New York: Guilford.

BEERS, KYLENE. 2003. *When Kids Can't Read What Teachers Can Do: A Guide for Teachers 6–12.* Portsmouth, NH: Heinemann.

BEERS, KYLENE, ROBERT PROBST, and LINDA RIEF, eds. 2007. *Adolescent Literacy: Turning Promise Into Practice.* Portsmouth, NH: Heinemann.

BENJAMIN, AMY. 2002. *Differentiated Instruction: A Guide for Middle and High School Teachers.* Poughkeepsie, NY: Eye on Education.

BIANCAROSA, GINA, and CATHERINE SNOW. 2004. *Reading Next: A Vision for Action and Research in Middle and High School Literacy.* New York: Carnegie Corporation.

BILLMEYER, RACHEL, and MARY LEE BARTON. 1998. *Teaching Reading in the Content Areas: If Not Me, Then Who?* Alexandria, VA: Association for Supervision and Curriculum Development.

BIRCHAK, BARB, CLAY CONNOR, KATHLEEN MARIE CRAWFORD, LESLIE KAHN, SANDY KASER, SUSAN TURNER, and KATHY SHORT. 1998. *Teacher Study Groups: Building Community Through Dialogue and Reflection.* Urbana, IL: National Council of Teachers of English.

CALDWELL, SARAH DEJARNETTE, ed. 1997. *Professional Development in Learning-Centered Schools.* Oxford, OH: National Staff Development Council.

CALHOUN, EMILY. 1993. "Action Research: Three Approaches." *Educational Leadership* (October): 13–16.

———. 2004. *Using Data to Assess Your Reading Program.* Alexandria, VA: Association for Supervision and Curriculum Development.

CAMBOURNE, BRIAN. 1988. *The Whole Story: Natural Learning and the Acquisition of Literacy in the Classroom.* New York: Scholastic.

———. 1995. "Toward an Educationally Relevant Theory of Literacy Learning: Twenty Years of Inquiry." *The Reading Teacher* 49 (November): 182–90.

COONEY, CAROLINE. 2004. *Code Orange.* New York: Delacorte Press.

COPELAND, MATT. 2005. *Socratic Circles: Fostering Critical Thinking in Middle and High Schools.* Portland, ME: Stenhouse.

COPELAND, MICHAEL, and MICHAEL KAPP. 2006. *Connecting Leadership with Learning: A Framework for Reflection, Planning, and Action.* Alexandria, VA: Association for Supervision and Curriculum Development.

COSTA, ARTHUR, and ROBERT GARMSTON. 2002. *Cognitive Coaching: A Foundation for Renaissance Schools.* Norwood, MA: Christopher-Gordon.

COVEY, STEPHEN. 1989. *The Seven Habits of Highly Effective People.* New York: Simon & Schuster.

CSIKSZENTMIHALYI, MIHALY. 1990. *Flow: The Psychology of Optimal Experience.* New York: Harper and Row.

DANIELS, HARVEY, and STEVEN ZEMELMAN. 2004. *Subjects Matter: Every Teacher's Guide to Content-Area Reading.* Portsmouth, NH: Heinemann.

DARLING-HAMMOND, LINDA, and GARY SYKES, eds. 1999. *Teaching as the Learning Profession: Handbook of Policy and Practice.* San Francisco: Jossey-Bass.

DOTY, JANE, GREGORY CAMERON, and MARY LEE BARTON. 2002. *Teaching Reading in Mathematics.* Alexandria, VA: Association for Supervision and Curriculum Development.

———. 2005. *Teaching Reading in Social Studies.* Alexandria, VA: Association for Supervision and Curriculum Development.

EAKER, ROBERT, RICHARD DuFOUR, and REBECCA DuFOUR. 2002. *Getting Started: Reculturing Schools to Become Professional Learning Communities.* Bloomington, IN: National Education Service.

ELBOW, PETER. 1973. *Writing Without Teachers.* New York: Oxford University Press.

ELLINOR, LINDA, and GLENNA GERARD. 1998. *Dialogue: Rediscover the Transforming Power of Conversation.* New York: John Wiley & Sons.

FULLAN, MICHAEL. 2003. *The Moral Imperative of School Leadership.* San Francisco: Jossey-Bass.

———. 2006. *Turnaround Leadership.* San Francisco: Jossey-Bass.

FULLAN, MICHAEL, PETER HILL, and CARMEL CREVOLA. 2006. *Breakthrough.* Thousand Oaks, CA: Corwin Press.

GARMSTON, ROBERT. 2006. "What Groups Talk About Matters — and *How* They Talk Matters, Too." *Journal of Staff Development* 27 (1): 73-74, 77.

GILMORE, BARRY. 2006. *Speaking Volumes: How to Get Students Discussing Books.* Portsmouth, NH: Heinemann.

GLANZ, JEFFREY. 2003. *Action Research: An Educational Leader's Guide to School Improvement.* 2nd ed. Norwood, MA: Christopher-Gordon.

GRAHAM, STEVE, and DELORES PERIN. 2007. *Writing Next: Effective Strategies to Improve Writing of Adolescents in Middle and High School.* New York: Carnegie Corporation.

GRAVES, MICHAEL. 2006. *The Vocabulary Book: Learning & Instruction.* New York: Teachers College Press.

GUSKEY, THOMAS. 2000. *Evaluating Professional Development.* Thousand Oaks, CA: Corwin Press.

GUTHRIE, JOHN, and DONNA ALVERMANN, eds. 1999. *Engaged Reading: Processes, Practices, and Policy Implications,* New York: Teachers College Press.

GUTHRIE, JOHN, and EMILY ANDERSON. 1999. Engagement in Reading: Processes of Motivated, Strategic, Knowledgeable, Social Readers. In *Engaged Reading: Processes, Practices, and Policy Implications,* ed. John Guthrie and Donna Alvermann, 17-45. New York: Teachers College Press.

HADDON, MARK. 2003. *The Curious Incident of the Dog in the Night-Time.* New York: Vintage Books.

HARGREAVES, ANDY. 1994. *Changing Teachers, Changing Times: Teachers' Work and Culture in the Postmodern Age.* New York: Teachers College Press.

———. 2006. "Teaching in the Knowledge Society." www.schoolsnetwork .org/uk/article.aspa?PageID=217469. Accessed December 28.

HARGREAVES, ANDY, and DEAN FINK. 2006. *Sustainable Leadership.* San Francisco: Jossey-Bass.

HARMON, JANIS. 2000. "Assessing and Supporting Independent Word Learning Strategies of Middle School Students." *Journal of Adult and Adolescent Literacy* 43 (6): 518-27.

HARP, BILL. 2000. *The Handbook of Literacy Assessment and Evaluation.* 2nd ed. Norwood, MA: Christopher-Gordon.

HORD, SHIRLEY. 2003. *Learning Together, Leading Together: Changing Schools Through Professional Learning Communities.* New York: Teachers College Press.

INTERNATIONAL READING ASSOCIATION and THE MIDDLE SCHOOL ASSOCIA- TION. 2001. *Supporting Young Adolescents' Literacy Learning: A Joint Po- sition Statement of the International Reading Association and the Mid- dle School Association.* Newark, DE: International Reading Association.

IRVIN, J. 1998. *Reading and the Middle School Student: Strategies to En- hance Literacy.* Boston: Allyn & Bacon.

———. 2001. "Assisting Struggling Readers in Building Vocabulary and Background Knowledge." *Voices from the Middle* 8 (4): 37-43.

IRVIN, JUDITH, DOUGLAS BUEHL, and RONALD KLEMP. 2003. *Reading and the High School Student: Strategies to Enhance Literacy.* Boston: Allyn & Bacon.

IVEY, GAY, and DOUGLAS FISHER. 2005. "Learning From What Doesn't Work." *Educational Leadership* 63 (2): 8–14.

———. 2006. *Creating Literacy-Rich Schools for Adolescents.* Alexandria, VA: Association for Supervision and Curriculum Development.

JENSEN, ERIC. 2006. *Enriching the Brain: How to Maximize Every Learner's Potential.* San Francisco: Jossey-Bass.

JOYCE, BRUCE, and BEVERLY SHOWERS, 1985. "Teachers Coaching Teachers." *Educational Leadership* 42 (117): 38–43.

———. 2002. *Student Achievement Through Staff Development.* 3rd ed. Alexandria, VA: Association for Supervision and Curriculum Development.

KNIGHT, JIM. 2007a. "5 Key Points to Building a Coaching Program." *Journal of Staff Development* 28(1): 26–31.

———. 2007b. *Instructional Coaching: A Partnership Approach to Improving Instruction.* Thousand Oaks, CA: Corwin Press.

LAMBERT, LINDA. 2003. *Leadership Capacity for Lasting School Improvement.* Alexandria, VA: Association for Supervision and Curriculum Development.

LANGER, GEORGEA, AMY COLTON, and LORETTA GOFF. 2003. *Collaborative Analysis of Student Work: Improving Teaching and Learning.* Alexandria, VA: Association for Supervision and Curriculum Development.

LENT, RELEAH. 2006a. "Creating a Culture for Writers." *Journal of Staff Development* 27 (3): 47–50.

———. 2006b. *Engaging Adolescent Learners: A Guide for Content-Area Teachers.* Portsmouth, NH: Heinemann.

LEVITT, STEVEN, and STEPHEN DUBNER. 2005. *Freakonomics: A Rogue Economist Explores the Hidden Side of Everything.* New York: Harper Collins.

LYONS, CAROL, and GAY SU PINNELL. 2001. *Systems for Change in Literacy Education: A Guide to Professional Development.* Portsmouth, NH: Heinemann.

MARZANO, ROBERT, DEBRA PICKERING, and JANE POLLOCK. 2001. *Classroom Instruction That Works: Research-Based Strategies for Increasing Student Achievement.* Alexandria, VA: Association for the Supervision and Curriculum Development.

MASLOW, ABRAHAM. 1954. *Motivation and Personality.* New York: Harper.

MEIER, DEBORAH. 2002. *In Schools We Trust: Creating Communities of Learning in an Era of Testing and Standardization.* Boston: Beacon Press.

MOORE, DAVID, THOMAS BEAN, DEANNER BIRDYSHAW, and JAMES RYCIK. 1999. *Adolescent Literacy: A Position Statement.* Newark, DE: International Reading Association.

MURPHY, CARLENE, and DALE LICK. 2001. *Whole-Faculty Study Groups: Creating Student-Based Professional Development.* 2nd ed. Thousand Oaks, CA: Corwin Press.

NAGY, WILLIAM. 1988. *Teaching Vocabulary to Improve Reading Comprehension.* Urbana, IL: National Council of Teachers of English.

NATIONAL COUNCIL OF TEACHERS OF ENGLISH. 2006. "NCTE Principals of Adolescent Literacy Reform: A Policy Research Brief." www.ncte.org.

NATIONAL RESEARCH COUNCIL. 2000. *How People Learn: Brain, Mind, Experience, and School.* Washington, DC: National Academy Press.

PALMER, PARKER. 1998. *The Courage to Teach: Exploring the Inner Landscape of a Teacher's Life.* San Francisco: Jossey-Bass.

PATTY, ANNA. 2006. "Students' Academic Success Can Be a Matter of Principal." *Sidney Morning Herald.* December 11. www.smh.com.

PILGREEN, J. J. 2001. *The SSR Handbook: How to Organize and Manage a Sustained Silent Reading Program.* Portsmouth, NH: Boynton/Cook.

PIPKIN, GLORIA, and RELEAH LENT. 2002. *At the Schoolhouse Gate: Lessons in Intellectual Freedom.* Portsmouth, NH: Heinemann.

PRESTON, RICHARD. 2002. *The Demon in the Freezer.* New York: Random House.

PUIG, ENRIQUE, and KATHY FROELICH. 2007. *The Literacy Coach: Guiding in the Right Direction.* Boston: Pearson Education.

RITCHHART, RON. 2002. *Intellectual Character: What Is It, Why It Matters, and How to Get It.* San Francisco: Jossey-Bass.

ROBB, LAURA. 2000. *Redefining Staff Development: A Collaborative Model for Teachers and Administrators.* Portsmouth, NH: Heinemann.

ROUTMAN, REGIE. 2002. "Teacher Talk." *Educational Leadership* 69 (6): 32–35.

RUDDELL, ROBERT, and BRENDA SHEARER. 2002. "'Extraordinary,' 'Tremendous,' 'Exhilarating,' 'Magnificent': Middle School At-Risk Students Become Avid Word Learners with the Vocabulary Self-Collection Strategy (VSS)." *Journal of Adolescent and Adult Literacy* 45 (5): 352–63.

RYCIK, JAMES, and JUDITH IRVIN. 2001. *What Adolescents Deserve: A Commitment to Students' Literacy Learning.* Newark, NJ: International Reading Association.

SAGOR, RICHARD. 1992. *How to Conduct Collaborative Action Research.* Alexandria, VA: Association for Supervision and Curriculum Development.

———. 2000. *Guiding School Improvement with Action Research.* Alexandria, VA: Association for Supervision and Curriculum Development.

SANDBURG, CARL. 1992. *Carl Sandburg: Selected Poems.* Avenel, NJ: Gramercy Books.

SCHOENBACH, RUTH, CYNTHIA GREENLEAF, CHRISTINE CZIKO, and LORI HURWITZ. 1995. *Reading for Understanding: A Guide to Improving Reading in Middle and High School Classrooms.* San Francisco: Jossey-Bass.

SENGE, PETER. 1990. *The Fifth Discipline: The Art and Practice of the Learning Organization.* New York: Doubleday.

SENGE, PETER, NELDA CAMBRON-MCCABE, TIMOTHY LUCAS, BRYAN SMITH, JANIS DUTTON, and ART KLEINER. 2000. *Schools That Learn: A Fifth Discipline Fieldbook for Educators, Parents, and Everyone Who Cares About Education.* New York: Doubleday.

SERGIOVANNI, THOMAS. 2004. *Strengthening the Heartbeat: Leading and Learning Together in Schools.* San Francisco: Jossey-Bass.

SHOWERS, BEVERLY, and BRUCE JOYCE. 1996. "The Evolution of Peer Coaching." *Educational Leadership* 53 (6):12–16.

SMITH, FRANK. 1998. *The Book of Learning and Forgetting.* New York: Teachers College Press.

SMITH, MICHAEL, and JEFFREY WILHELM. 2006. *Going with the Flow: How to Engage Boys (and Girls) in Their Literacy Learning.* Portsmouth, NH: Heinemann.

SOUTHWEST EDUCATIONAL DEVELOPMENT LABORATORY. 1997. "Professional Learning Communities: What Are They and Why Are They Important?" *Issues . . . About Change.* www.sedl.org/change/issues/issue61.html.

SPARKS, DENNIS. 2002. *Designing Powerful Professional Development for Teachers and Principals.* Oxford, OH: National Staff Development Council.

SPIEGELMAN, ART. 1991. *Maus: A Survivor's Tale I and II.* New York: Pantheon Books.

STIGGINS, RICHARD. 2001. *Student-Involved Classroom Assessment.* 3rd ed. Columbus, OH: Merrill Prentice Hall.

TOMLINSON, CAROL ANN. 2003. *Fulfilling the Promise of the Differentiated Classroom: Strategies and Tools for Responsive Teaching.* Alexandria, VA: Association for Supervision and Curriculum Development.

TOVANI, CRIS. 2004. *Do I Really Have to Teach Reading?: Content, Comprehension, Grades 6–12.* Portland, ME: Stenhouse.

TSCHANNEN-MORAN, MEGAN. 2004. *Trust Matters: Leadership for Successful Schools.* San Francisco: Jossey-Bass.

WALLIS, CLAUDIA, and SONJA STEPTOE. 2006. "How to Bring Our Schools Out of the 20th Century." *Time* 18 (December): 50–56.

WARLICK, DAVID, 2004. *Redefining Literacy for the 21st Century.* Worthington, OH: Linworth.

WHITE, STEPHEN. 2005. *Beyond the Numbers: Making Data Work for Teachers and School Leaders.* Oxford, OH: National Staff Development Council.

WILHELM, JEFFREY. 2007. *Engaging Readers and Writers with Inquiry: Promoting Deep Understandings in Language Arts and the Content Areas with Guiding Questions.* New York: Scholastic.

"Will High Schools Be a Relic of the Past?" 2007. CBS News. January 4. www.cbsnews.com/stories/2006/12/28/eveningnews/main2307635 .shtml.

WILSON, MAJA. 2006. *Rethinking Rubrics in Writing Assessment.* Portsmouth, NH: Heinemann.

WOLFE, PATRICIA. 2001. *Brain Matters: Translating Research into Classroom Practice.* Alexandria, VA: Association for Supervision and Curriculum Development.

ZARNOWSKI, MYRA. 2006. *Making Sense of History: Using High-Quality Literature and Hands-on Experiences to Build Content Knowledge.* New York: Scholastic.

ZULL, JAMES. 2002. *The Art of Changing the Brain: Enriching the Practice of Teaching by Exploring the Biology of Learning.* Sterling, VA: Stylus.

# *Index*